AREA STUDIES

North and South America

David Waugh

Head of the Geography Department
Trinity School, Carlisle

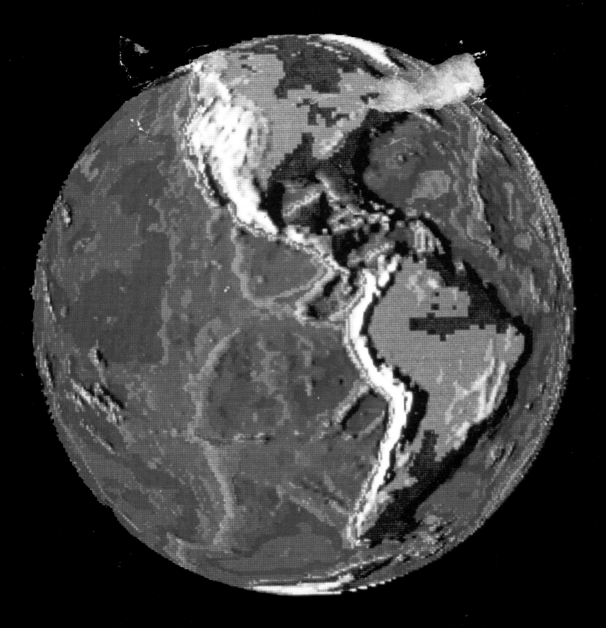

Nelson

Thomas Nelson and Sons Ltd
Nelson House   Mayfield Road
Walton-on-Thames   Surrey
KT12 5PL   UK

51 York Place
Edinburgh
EH1 3JD   UK

Thomas Nelson (Hong Kong) Ltd
Toppan Building 10/F
22A Westlands Road
Quarry Bay   Hong Kong

Distributed in Australia by

Thomas Nelson Australia
102 Dodds Street
South Melbourne
Victoria 3205   Australia

© David Waugh 1984
First published by Thomas Nelson & Sons Ltd 1984
ISBN 0-17-434175-X
NPN 19 18 17 16 15 14 13 12 11

Title page photograph supplied by Science Photo Library and shows a topographic map of North and South America. Each colour corresponds to an elevation interval of 500 metres.

The author and publishers are grateful to the following for permission to use their photographs:

K. Ackford Figs. 1.2, 2.16, 14.16; Aerofilms Figs. 5.7, 13.20; M. Andrews Figs. 1.12, 2.13, 2.14; Associated Press Fig. 1.18; Anne Bolt Fig. 11.8; R. Brook Fig. 8.2; Canada House Figs. 6.29, 9.6, 9.9, 10.16, 11.5, 13.23, 13.29; J. Allan Cash Figs. 2.17, 10.3; Colorific Figs. 1.15, 1.20, 1.21, 2.25, 3.10, 5.3, 5.19, 6.11, 6.25, 9.11, 10.8, 10.13, 10.14, 13.10, 13.12, 13.16, 14.15, 15.2, 17.14; Cunards Fig. 14.24; James Davis Fig. 14.16; Earthscan Figs. 8.5, 8.9; Geological Survey of Canada Fig. 11.7; Mike Goldwater/ Network Fig. 10.21; Sally & Richard Greenhill Figs. 3.3, 5.10, 5.13, 6.19; Susan Griggs Agency Fig. 12.3; Robert Harding Figs. 1.3, 2.18, 2.19, 2.28, 2.29, 4.12, 14.13, 5.3 (mid.), 5.18, 5.23, 6.24, 8.14, 9.7, 9.8, 9.10, 10.19, 11.3, 13.4, 13.5, 13.6, 13.14, 13.25, 14.3, 14.4, 14.5, 14.7, 14.16, (lwr.), 17.5; Alan Hutchinson Figs. 1.24, 2.2, 2.5, 2.8, 2.15, 2.20, 2.21, 2.25, 3.3, 3.3, 3.14, 5.15, 5.16, 5.20, 6.7, 6.8, 6.9, 6.10, 6.21, 6.22, 9.3, 11.2, 12.7, 13.2, 13.3, 13.7, 13.19, 13.30, 14.19 (both); ICI Fig. 12.13; Keystone Press Agency Figs. 2.10, 2.11, 15.9; Frank Lane Fig. 2.24; Mississippi Department of Agriculture and Commerce Fig. 6.15; Peter Newarks Western Americana Fig. 1.18; Nova Scotia House Fig. 13.27; Nova Scotia Power Corporation Fig. 10.18; Picturepoint Figs. 2.22, 5.25, 6.13, 6.16, 8.15, 10.2, 15.12; David Simson Figs 2.4, 5.9, 5.14, 17.6; South American Pictures Fig. 9.4; Speed Bird Holidays Figs. 14.22, 14.23; Sporting Pictures Fig. 3.13; Texaco Fig. 10.6; Via Rail Fig. 13.11; R. E. Wallace, US Geological Survey Fig. 1.17; Val Wilmer Figs. 3.3, 5.12.

We are indebted to the following for permission to produce diagrams based on copyright materials:

John Barholomen & Son Ltd. (from World Environmental Problems by Norman Thomson); Heinemann Educational Books (from North America: A New Geography by S. Dunlop and D. MacDonald); Methuen and Co., and G. Barber (from An Atlas of North American Affairs by D. K. Adams, S. F. Mills and H. B. Rodgers); Oliver and Boyd (from Geographical Studies in North America by B. E. Price and E. Tweed); Population Concern; The Director, Institute of Geological Sciences (NERC), Crown Copyright reserved; The Geographical Association (from Geography); The Geographical Magazine; United Nations Fund for Population Activities.

Maps suplied by Swanston Graphics, Derby

Diagrams supplied by Maltings Partnership, Duffield

Printed and bound in Hong Kong

Contents

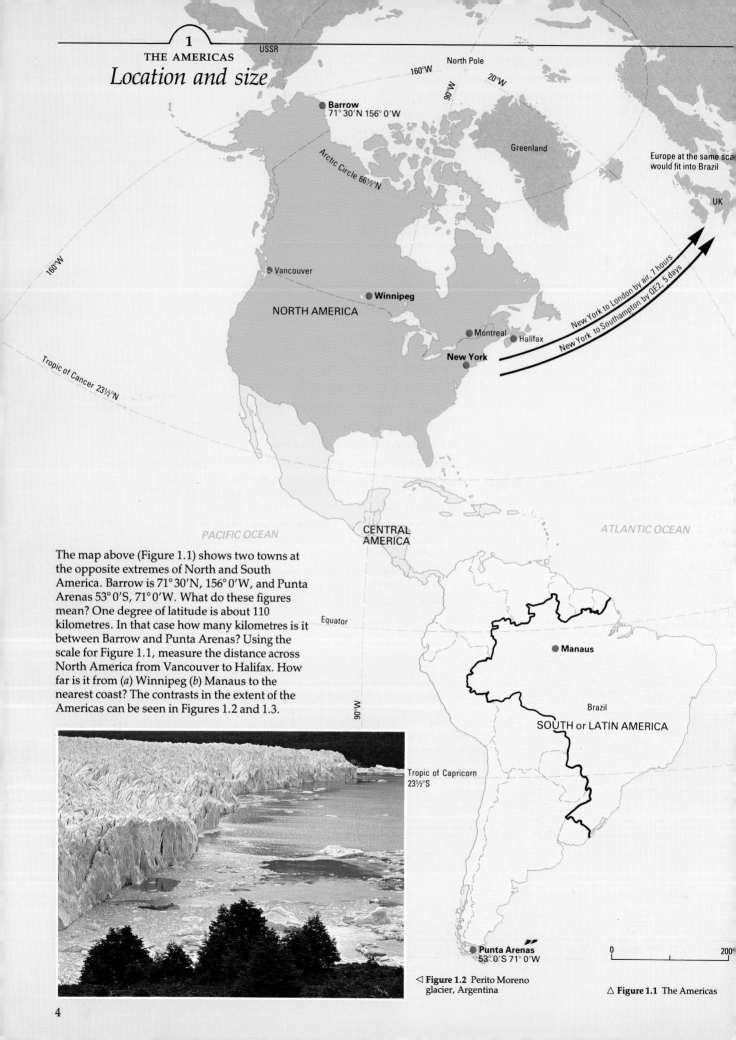

USSR

160°W

North Pole

20°W

90°W

Barrow
71° 30'N 156° 0'W

Greenland

Arctic Circle 66½°N

Europe at the same sca
would fit into Brazil

UK

160°W

Vancouver

Winnipeg

NORTH AMERICA

Montreal

Halifax

New York

New York to London by air, 7 hours

New York to Southampton by QE2, 5 days

Tropic of Cancer 23½°N

PACIFIC OCEAN

CENTRAL
AMERICA

ATLANTIC OCEAN

The map above (Figure 1.1) shows two towns at
the opposite extremes of North and South
America. Barrow is 71° 30'N, 156° 0'W, and Punta
Arenas 53° 0'S, 71° 0'W. What do these figures
mean? One degree of latitude is about 110
kilometres. In that case how many kilometres is it
between Barrow and Punta Arenas? Using the
scale for Figure 1.1, measure the distance across
North America from Vancouver to Halifax. How
far is it from (a) Winnipeg (b) Manaus to the
nearest coast? The contrasts in the extent of the
Americas can be seen in Figures 1.2 and 1.3.

Equator

● **Manaus**

Brazil

SOUTH or LATIN AMERICA

90°W

Tropic of Capricorn
23½°S

0   200

Punta Arenas
53° 0'S 71° 0'W

◁ **Figure 1.2** Perito Moreno
glacier, Argentina

△ **Figure 1.1** The Americas

◁ **Figure 1.3** Amazon rainforest, Brazil

Figure 1.4 is an extract from a United States train timetable. Although the journeys between New York and Los Angeles actually take about 60 hours, it can be seen that the journey from New York is timetabled to take considerably less than that from Los Angeles. Why is this?

The earth rotates through its 360° of longitude every 24 hours, and places in the east receive daylight before places in the west.

$$\frac{24 \text{ hours}}{360°} = 1 \text{ hour time difference for every } 15° \text{ of longitude.}$$

As a result the world is divided into a series of time zones, each approximately 15° in longitude. Figure 1.5 shows how Canada and the USA are divided.

1 How many hours ahead is Halifax compared with Vancouver?

2 Why is Halifax ahead of Vancouver?

3 Why are the lines dividing time zones not always straight (e.g., those between Atlantic Standard Time and Eastern Standard Time)?

4 If it is lunchtime in Halifax, what meal would someone be eating at that time in (a) London (b) Vancouver?

5 If you flew between New York and Los Angeles by a non-stop jet, why would it be possible to have two breakfasts?

6 What is jet lag?

Figure 1.4 Extract from a United States AMTRAK timetable (below left)

▽ **Figure 1.5** Time zones in North America

Route: New York – Chicago – Kansas City – Los Angeles
Services: restaurant, sleeping accommodation and medical
Frequency: Daily

read down		km	miles	station	read up	
day	time				day	time
Mon.	14.15	0	0	New York	Thurs.	16.37
Mon.	14.32	16	10	Newark	Thurs.	16.20
Mon.	15.51	145	90	Philadelphia	Thurs.	14.46
Mon.	17.55	310	192	Harrisburg	Thurs.	12.52
Mon.	23.17	710	441	Pittsburgh	Thurs	06.48
Tues.	09.05*	1463	909	Chicago	Wed.	20.00
Tues.	15.45			Chicago	Wed.	15.15*
Tues.	23.20	2188	1360	Kansas City	Wed.	06.30
Wed.	01.00	2294	1425	Topeka	Wed.	05.05
Wed.	15.15	3637	2260	Albuquerque	Tues.	12.50
Thurs.	07.20	5067	3149	Los Angeles	Mon.	19.40
	58.25		timetable journey time			64.12

*Change trains

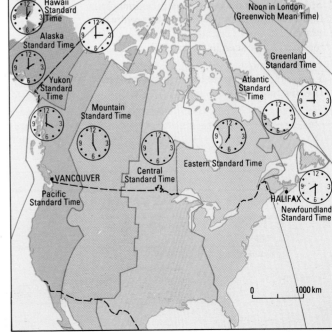

Plate tectonics

The earth's crust, which, if the earth were the size of an apple, would be no thicker than the apple's skin, can be divided into seven large plates and several smaller ones (Figure 1.6).

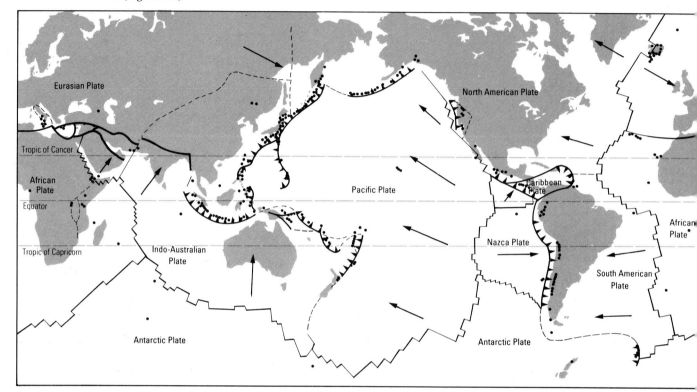

Because of heat from within the earth, these plates move either towards, away from, or sideways relative to surrounding plates. It is at plate boundaries that most of the world's major landforms occur, and where earthquake, volcanic and mountain building zones are located. It must be remembered, however, that:

☐ Most changes take place at plate boundaries, and very little change occurs in the centre of plates.

☐ No gaps can occur on the earth's surface so, if two plates move apart, new oceanic crust must form, originating from underneath the crust (i.e. the mantle).

☐ Plates cannot overlap, which means that either they must be pushed up on impact to form mountains, or one must be forced downwards and destroyed.

☐ Continental crust cannot sink, whereas oceanic crust, being heavier, can.

☐ Continental plates, such as the North American, can include both continental and oceanic crust.

The last two points refer to the two main types of crust; the differences between them are given in Figure 1.7. Plates can move in three directions in relation to other plates, and these movements and resultant landforms are summarised in Figure 1.8. Figure 1.9 shows how an understanding of plate tectonics accounts for the major relief features of the Americas.

:•·:•·:	volcanoes	
▲▲▲▲▲	subduction zone	
- - - - -	uncertain plate boundaries	
⟶	movement of plate	
⌐⌐⌐⌐	spreading ridge offset by transform faults	
⎯⎯⎯	collision zone	

△ **Figure 1.6** Plate boundaries and active zones of the earth's crust

◁ **Figure 1.7** Differences between continental and oceanic crust

	Continental Crust	Oceanic Crust
thickness	35 to 70 km on average	6 to 10 km
age of rocks	very old, mainly over 1500 million years	very young, mainly under 200 million years
weight of rocks	lighter with an average density of 2.6	heavier with an average density of 3.0
nature of rocks	light in colour numerous types many contain silica and oxygen granite is the most common	dark in colour few types, mainly basalt

pe of plate boundary	description of changes	examples from the Americas
Constructive margins (spreading plates)	Two plates move away from each other New oceanic crust appears forming mid ocean ridges with volanoes	Mid-Atlantic Ridge, (Americas moving away from Eurasia, Africa) East Pacific Rise, (Nazca and Pacific plates moving apart)
Destructive margins (subduction zones)	Oceanic crust moves towards continental crust but being heavier sinks and is destroyed forming deep sea trenches and volcanic island arcs Activity; often mountain building on continental fringe	Nazca sinks under South America plate (Andes) Juan de Fuca sinks under North America plate (Rockies) Island arcs of the West Indies and Aleutians
Conservative or passive margins (transform faults)	Two plates move sideways past each other, land is neither formed nor destroyed	San Andreas fault in California
B. centres of plates are rigid	Rigid plate centres form i) shield lands of ancient worn down rocks ii) depressions on edges of the shields, developing into large river basins	 Canadian (Laurentian) Shield, Brazilian Sheild Mississippi-Missouri, Amazon, Parana

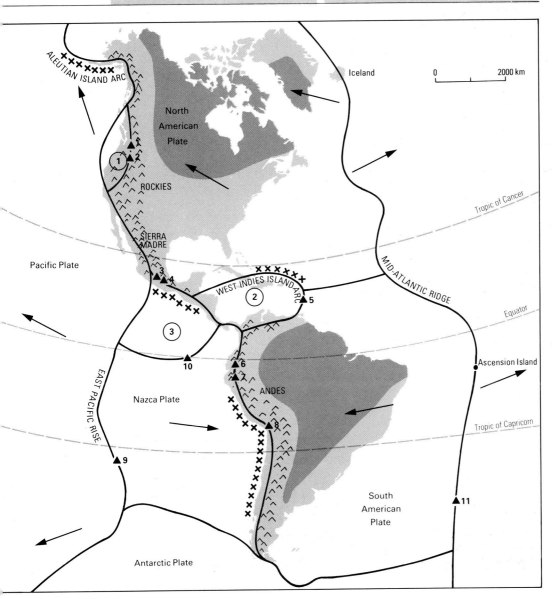

1 Juan de Fuca Plate
2 Caribbean Plate
3 Cocos Plate

↗ direction of plate movement

volcanoes
1 Rainier
2 Mt St Helens
3 Paricutin
4 Popocatepetl
5 Mt Pelée
6 Cotopaxi
7 Chimborazo
8 El Misti
9 Easter Island
10 Galapagos Island
11 Tristan da Cunha

×××× deep sea trenches

▨ shield lands

ʌʌʌʌ young fold mountains

— plate boundaries

◁ **Figure 1.9** The Americas – plates and major relief features

Figure 1.8 lists three types of plate boundaries.

Constructive margins

At constructive margins, such as the Mid-Atlantic Ridge (Figure 1.10), two plates move away from each other. Molten rock, or magma, immediately rises to fill any possible 'gap' and so new rocks are formed. The Atlantic Ocean is widening by about 9 centimetres a year, which means that not only are the Americas moving away from Eurasia and Africa, but they are also moving towards such plates as the Nazca, Cocos and Juan de Fuca (Figure 1.9).

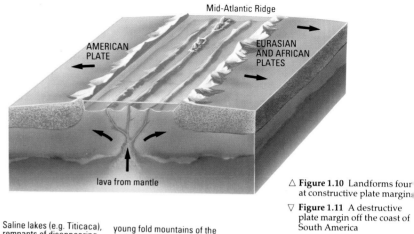

△ **Figure 1.10** Landforms four at constructive plate margin

▽ **Figure 1.11** A destructive plate margin off the coast of South America

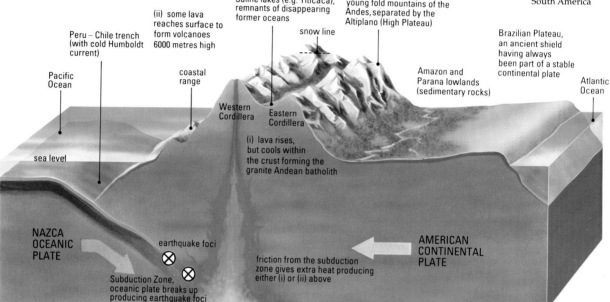

Destructive margins

Off South America, the Nazca plate is moving towards the American plate (Figure 1.11). Since oceanic crust cannot override continental crust, the Nazca plate dips downwards to form a subduction zone with an associated deep sea trench (the Peru-Chile trench). As this plate descends it takes part of the oceanic crust back into the mantle and the resultant friction causes both severe earth movements (earthquakes) and an increase in temperature. Being less dense than the mantle, the now molten former oceanic crust will rise towards the earth's surface. This in turn can produce different types of surface landforms.

☐ If, as in South America, the subduction zone borders a continent, the molten material will form a chain of volcanoes (e.g. Cotopaxi, Chimborazo, Sangay and Llaima – Figure 1.12) in a long, high mountain chain (e.g. the Andes) into which may be later injected masses of molten granite (the Andean batholith) which will metamorphose existing crustal rocks.

☐ If the lava rises towards the surface still under the ocean it creates a chain of volcanic off-shore islands (an island arc) such as in the West Indies and the Aleutians (Figures 1.9 and 1.13).

△ **Figure 1.12** Llaima volcano in the Andean mountain range, Chile

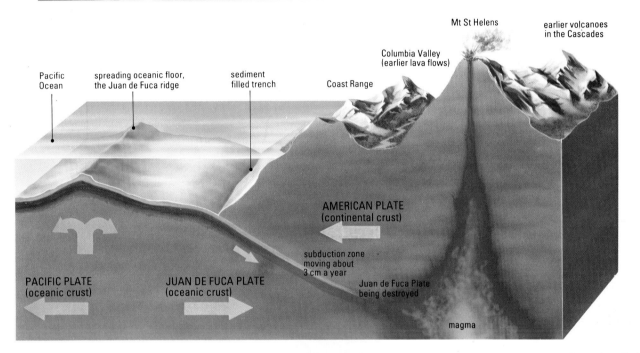

The Mount St Helens eruption (Figure 1.15) On 20 March 1980 the first major earthquake, measuring 4.1 on the Richter scale, occurred and on 27 March the first eruption of ash took place. Figure 1.14 attempts to explain the cause of the eruption.

◁ **Figure 1.13** Island arcs

▽ **Figure 1.14** The Mount St Helens eruption

After a month of increasing activity, it was noted that the whole northern face of the volcano appeared to be swelling, and *'at 8.32 a.m. on May 18th two geologists were circling the summit . . . in a light aircraft, taking photographs of the snow-covered inactive crater when, to their horror, the whole northern side of the mountain began to move . . . Seconds later, a massive cloud of ash began to mushroom upwards, climbing tens of thousands of metres into the air. . . .*

'The eruption sent hot gas and black ash towering 15 km above the volcano, blotting out the sun for more than 150 km. At least five persons were killed, 21 were missing and Spirit Lake at the base of the mountain disappeared under rock and mudflows.

'Bolts of lightning sparked forest fires over thousands of acres. Mudflows and floods poured down the mountain, destroying bridges and forcing the evacuation of some 2,000 people. After a quiet spell, the volcano erupted again in early 1982.' (Geographical Magazine, August 1982)

◁ **Figure 1.15** Mount St Helens

THE AMERICAS

Landforms

Conservative margins

The San Andreas Fault runs through California (Figures 1.16 and 1.17). It marks the boundary between the American and Pacific plates. Although the American fault is almost stationary at this point, the Pacific plate is moving by about 6 centimetres a year. These two plates should slip past each other but they tend, like a machine without oil, to stick until pressure builds up enabling one plate to jerk forwards, sending shockwaves throughout the surrounding countryside. In 1906 at San Francisco the ground moved by 6 metres in an earthquake which measured 7.9 on the Richter scale.

At 5.12 a.m. on April 18th 1906 the ground began to shake. There were three tremors, each one increasingly more severe. Many apartments collapsed but few people were killed. Then came the fire; it started in numerous places resulting from overturned stoves, or sparked by electricity or the ignition of gas escaping from the broken mains. For 52 fires there were only 38 horse-drawn fire engines, and most watermains were fractured. It took 3 days to put out the fires by which time 450 people had died, 28,000 buildings had been destroyed and an area six times greater than that destroyed by the Great Fire of London had been ravaged.

But San Francisco was rebuilt and by the 1980s housed almost 5 million people. However, in recent years there has been little movement on the fault, and it is suggested that it is about 4 metres behind schedule. One day soon it is feared that this 4 metres will be made up. Will this destroy San Francisco or another Californian city? Will there be another fire? Or will tidal waves swamp coastal cities?

However, should the 6 centimetres a year movement resume and continue, eventually there will come a time when Los Angeles will lie as far to the north of San Francisco as it now lies to the south (Figure 1.16).

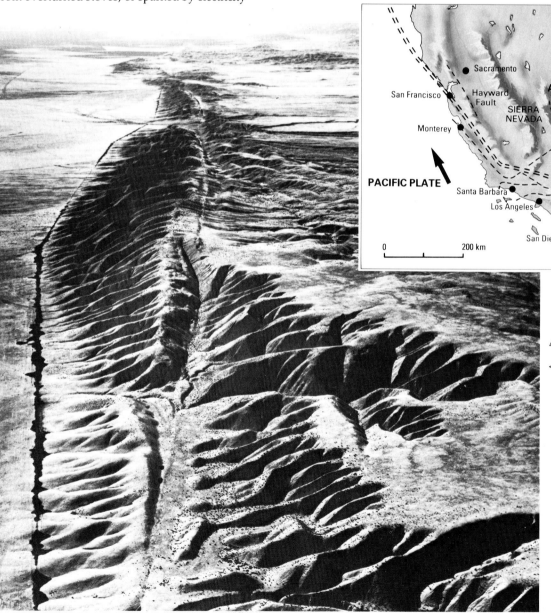

△ **Figure 1.16** Location of the San Andreas Fault

◁ **Figure 1.17** The San Andreas Fault

VALDEZ 1964

e town of Valdez was hit by an earthquake
easuring 8.6 on the Richter Scale on Good Friday
64. A submarine landslide carried away the
rbour and caused tidal waves which swept into
e town. Most of the 115 deaths were due to
owning. Afterwards Valdez was relocated several
ometres to the west on firmer ground, and rebuilt.
ing earthquake-resistant features. Valdez is now
e all year round ice-free port at the terminus of the
ans-Alaska oil pipeline (see page 121).

OUNT ST HELENS 1980

people killed or missing in volcanic eruption
ich was 500 times the power of the Hiroshima
mb. Two million mammals, birds and fish killed.

EUREKA 1980

Six people were injured in 1980 when this highway
south of Eureka collapsed in an early morning
earthquake. The railway below was blocked for
some time by falling debris.

AN FRANCISCO 1906

rthquake and fire caused 500 deaths.

EL CHINCHONAL 1982

Volcano erupted in 1982 killing 21 people, injuring 500
and causing 60 000 others to be evacuated. Those
rescued were suffering from burns, dehydration,
breathing problems and malnutrition. Army para-
troopers took several days to reach isolated villages
cut off by ash over a metre thick.

MARTINIQUE 1902

During early stages of the Mt Pelée eruption clouds
of red hot cinders and a stench of sulphur filled the
air. All but two of the 30 000 inhabitants of St Pierre
died in the major eruption. The volcano exploded into
a solid wall of flame which rolled over the city. A
wave of heat and gases killed thousands instan-
taneously, and within seconds the city was stripped
of every landmark.

ARICUTIN 1943

gan as a crack in a cornfield, within a year a
arby village was buried by ash. By 1952 when the
uption stopped five towns had been resettled and
ricutin was 410 metres high.

UATEMALA 1976

rthquake caused 23 000 deaths and made one
lion homeless

NICARAGUA 1972

Earthquake caused 12 000 deaths

Figure 1.18 Twentieth
century natural disasters
resulting from plate
movements in the
Americas

PERU 1970

Several villages wiped out by huge mud avalanches
following a major earthquake which measured 7.7 on
the Richter Scale. 20 000 lost.

estruction of San Francisco 1906

Mt Pelée, Martinique 1902

Side effects

1 Avalanches

In 1970 an earthquake recording 7.7 on the Richter scale shook parts of Peru north of the capital, Lima. The shock waves loosened a mass of ice and snow near the summit of Huascaran, the highest peak in the country (Figure 1.19). As the ice and snow fell 3000 metres it picked up rocks and boulders and the avalanche hit the town of Yungay at an estimated 480 kilometres per hour. When rescue workers eventually reached the area three days later, they found very few survivors out of a population of over 20 000 and only the tops of several 30 metre palm trees marking the spot of the former town square. In this earthquake the port of Chimbote was ruined, but at Yungay nature had already buried its victims (Figure 1.20).

◁ **Figure 1.19** Location of Huascaran and Yungay, Peru

△ **Figure 1.20** Yungay – all that remained of the town after the earthquake

▽ **Figure 1.21** Kodiak, Alaska, after the tidal wave

2 Tsunamis (tidal waves)

These are caused by the rapid uplift or depression of the ocean floor during an earthquake. Surface waves are formed which may only be a metre or two in height, but which can travel at about 750 kilometres per hour. In mid-ocean these are insignificant, but as they approach the shelving coastline of the land, the waves can rise to heights of over 12 metres and can cause loss of life and destruction.

In 1964, off the south coast of Alaska, an earthquake appeared to open the sea-bed and most of the inshore water disappeared, only to be replaced by a huge tidal wave. Figure 1.21 shows the effect of this wave on the port of Kodiak (notice the position of the largest ship).

The largest recorded tsunami followed an earthquake near Valdivia in Central Chile in 1960. Waves reached the Hawaiian islands, 10 000 kilometres away, in 15 hours, and Japan, 17 000 kilometres away, in 24 hours.

It is tidal waves which cause the greatest loss of life in coastal zones affected by earthquakes.

3 Benefits

Mineral wealth It was the mineral wealth and the dreams of El Dorado that enticed many explorers, especially Spaniards, to the 'New World'. For a long period before this present century, almost all the world's gold and silver came from mines developed in the volcanic rocks of the fold mountains bordering the Pacific Ocean, where many a prospector made his fortune (or lost it). Even today large amounts of the world's gold, silver, copper, lead, zinc and sulphur come from this area (Figure 1.22).

Leading world producers in the Americas

Copper 1 USA (2 USSR) 3 Chile 4 Canada

Silver (1 USSR) 2 Mexico 3 Peru 4 Canada 5 USA

Tin (1 Malaysia) 2 Bolivia

Lead (1 USSR) 2 USA (3 Australia) 4 Canada 5 Mexico 6 Peru

Fertile soils Although the first falls of ash from an erupting volcano will kill off all crops, the ash, which is composed of fine glassy particles, is easily weathered into a rich soil full of such elements as potassium. This may lead to high crop yields (e.g. coffee areas of Costa Rica, Guatemala and Colombia) and attract high population densities.

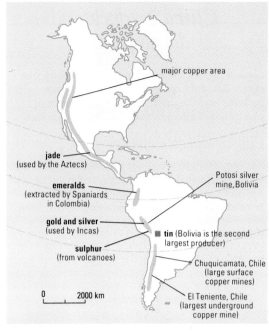

△ **Figure 1.22** Location of minerals formed near plate boundaries

significant deposits of copper, gold and silver, plus some lead, zinc and sulphur

▽ **Figure 1.23** Geothermal heat

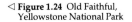

Geothermal heat Figure 1.23 illustrates how electricity can be obtained from the heated rocks if they are near enough to the earth's surface. Small schemes operate in California and northern Chile as well as in Nicaragua and El Salvador (page 83).

Fishing The upwelling of cold water from the Peru-Chile deep sea trench encourages the growth of fish food and therefore fish. Peru is a major fishing country (page 61).

Tourism The spectacular mountain scenery with its volcanoes and geysers (Figure 1.24) attracts both those who wish to look at attractive views and those who are more active and enjoy climbing and walking. National parks have been created in an attempt to preserve this beauty and recreational resource (page 108).

◁ **Figure 1.24** Old Faithful, Yellowstone National Park

Climate zones and development

Look at each of the ten climate graphs shown in Figure 2.1 and explain how the temperature patterns and the distribution and amounts of precipitation affect human activity in each area.

Climate and development

It is important to recognise that those areas in the world which suffer from the greatest handicaps of a hostile climate and poor soils tend to be the poorest countries of the developing world. Such countries, which usually lie within the tropics, suffer from:

☐ High annual temperatures, averaging over 20°C.

☐ Inadequate rainfall, excessive rainfall, or both at different seasons of the year.

☐ Poor health, because the heat provides ideal incubating conditions for diseases and insect carriers which can affect humans, animals and crops.

☐ Poor soils, because the heat breaks up humus faster than it can form, and the resultant poor soil structure cannot hold water.

☐ Heavy rainfall which leaches out nutrients and washes the topsoil away.

☐ Insufficient water supply in dry areas for plant growth and domestic needs.

☐ Strong winds which can ruin crops, destroy property and blow topsoil away.

climate	vegetation
1 Equatorial	tropical rainforests with coastal mangrove swamps
2 Tropical climates	
2A Savanna	tropical grasslands
2B Desert and semi-desert	scrub, sage bush and cacti
2C Trade wind coasts	tropical rainforests
3 Warm temperate climates	
3A Mediterranean (west coasts)	evergreen forests with chapparal
3B East coasts	deciduous forest
4 Cool temperate climates	
4A Western margins	mixed forests
4B Eastern margins	deciduous forests
4C Interior (continental)	temperate prairie grassland
4D Semi-desert	scrub
5 Cold climates	coniferous forest
6 Arctic climates	tundra
7 Mountains	Andean Tierras

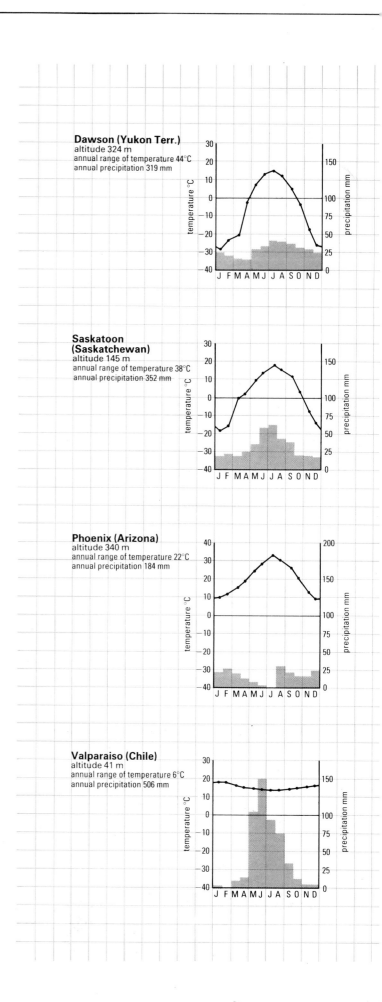

Figure 2.1 Climate and vegetation zones in the Americas

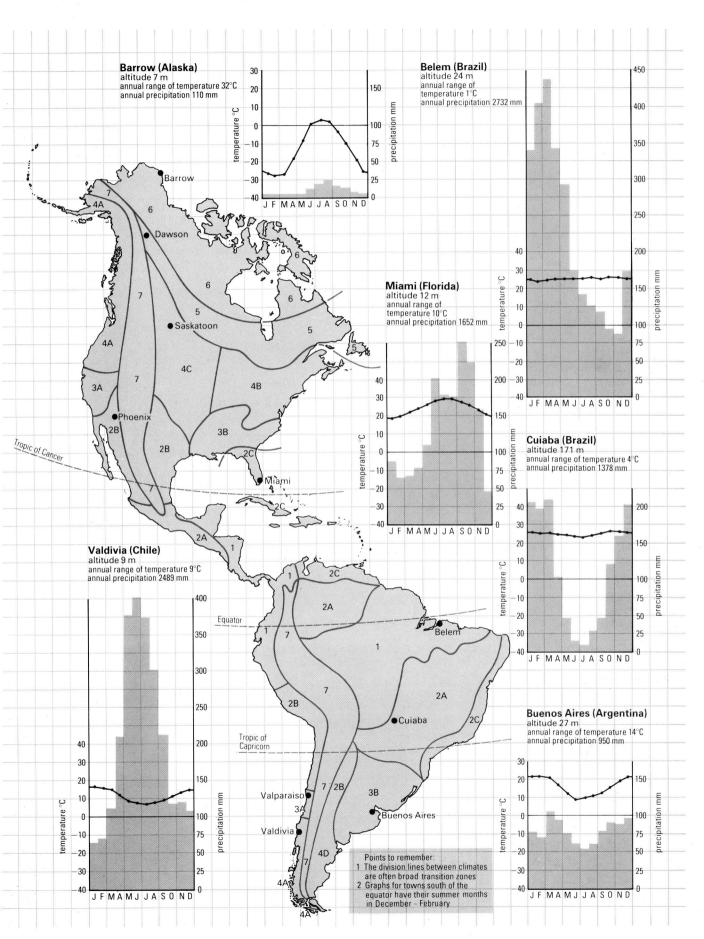

Barrow (Alaska)
altitude 7 m
annual range of temperature 32°C
annual precipitation 110 mm

Belem (Brazil)
altitude 24 m
annual range of
temperature 1°C
annual precipitation 2732 mm

Miami (Florida)
altitude 12 m
annual range of
temperature 10°C
annual precipitation 1652 mm

Cuiaba (Brazil)
altitude 171 m
annual range of temperature 4°C
annual precipitation 1378 mm

Valdivia (Chile)
altitude 9 m
annual range of temperature 9°C
annual precipitation 2489 mm

Buenos Aires (Argentina)
altitude 27 m
annual range of temperature 14°C
annual precipitation 950 mm

Barrow

Dawson

Saskatoon

Phoenix

Miami

Tropic of Cancer

Valparaiso

Valdivia

Buenos Aires

Cuiaba

Belem

Equator

Tropic of Capricorn

Points to remember:
1 The division lines between climates are often broad transition zones
2 Graphs for towns south of the equator have their summer months in December – February

Equatorial

As the graph (Figure 2.1) for Belem shows, the climate is hot all year (small annual range), rainfall is heavy (over 2000 mm) and there is neither a cool nor a really dry season. This, together with a constant high humidity, makes these areas unhealthy for humans. The location of areas experiencing this climate is shown on the map in Figure 2.1.

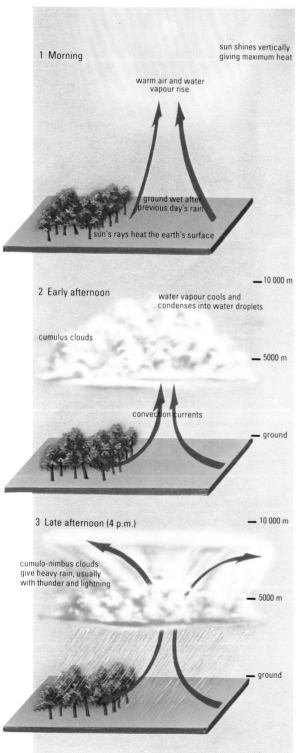

1 Morning

sun shines vertically giving maximum heat

warm air and water vapour rise

ground wet after previous day's rain

sun's rays heat the earth's surface

— 10 000 m

2 Early afternoon

water vapour cools and condenses into water droplets

cumulus clouds

— 5000 m

convection currents

— ground

3 Late afternoon (4 p.m.)

— 10 000 m

cumulo-nimbus clouds give heavy rain, usually with thunder and lightning

— 5000 m

— ground

The daily rhythm

One day is very similar to another throughout the year. The sun rises about 0600 hours and its heat soon evaporates the morning mists, the heavy dew, and the moisture remaining from the previous afternoon's storm. Even by 0800 hours the temperatures are as high as 25°C. As the sun rises to a near vertical position, temperatures exceed 33°C, and water from swamps, the numerous rivers and the forest is evaporated. Strong upward convection currents (Figure 2.2) lift the vapour high into the sky until it reaches cooler altitudes. When the rising air is cooled to its dew point (the temperature at which water vapour condenses into droplets of water) large, towering cumulus clouds develop. By mid-afternoon these clouds have turned black and produce torrential downpours which are usually accompanied by thunder and lightning. These storms soon cease but the air remains calm and humid. By the time the sun sets, always about 1800 hours, the clouds have already broken up. Such conditions are similar through the year, seemingly one long tropical day.

Equatorial rainforests

One in every ten trees covering the earth's surface grows in the Amazon Basin.

How does the vegetation adapt to the climate?
(Figure 2.4)

☐ The forest has an evergreen appearance due to the continuous growing season (Figure 2.3). This means that trees can shed leaves at any time.

☐ The trees can reach over 40 metres in their efforts to get sunlight (Figure 2.4).

☐ The rainforest is the most luxuriant vegetation system in the world because of constant high temperatures and the abundance of rain (Figure 2.5).

◁ **Figure 2.2** Daily convectional rainfall

▽ **Figure 2.3** River Amazon flowing through the equatorial rainforest, Brazil

△ **Figure 2.4** Adaptation of vegetation to an equatorial climate. Vegetation grows in distinct layers – the lowest layer consisting of shrubs where sunlight penetrates the tree layer, the under canopy, the main canopy, and the emergents which grow to over 40 m to reach the sunlight

emergents

main canopy

under canopy

shrub layer

The natural tropical forest

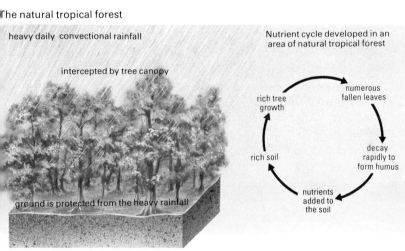

heavy daily convectional rainfall

intercepted by tree canopy

ground is protected from the heavy rainfall

Nutrient cycle developed in an area of natural tropical forest

numerous fallen leaves → decay rapidly to form humus → nutrients added to the soil → rich soil → rich tree growth → numerous fallen leaves

The cleared tropical forest

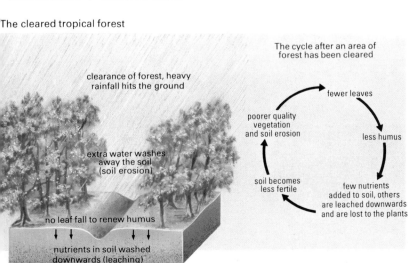

clearance of forest, heavy rainfall hits the ground

extra water washes away the soil (soil erosion)

no leaf fall to renew humus

nutrients in soil washed downwards (leaching)

The cycle after an area of forest has been cleared

fewer leaves → less humus → few nutrients added to soil, others are leached downwards and are lost to the plants → soil becomes less fertile → poorer quality vegetation and soil erosion → fewer leaves

◁ **Figure 2.6** The forest cycle   △ **Figure 2.5** The equatorial rainforest, Brazil

- ☐ The leaves have drip tips to shed the heavy rainfall.
- ☐ Large buttress roots stand above the ground to give support to the trees.
- ☐ Lianas, which are vine-like plants, use large trees as a support to climb up to the canopy.
- ☐ As only about 1 per cent of the incoming sunlight reaches the forest floor, there is little undergrowth.
- ☐ Fallen leaves soon decay in the hot, wet climate.
- ☐ Tree trunks are straight and, in their lower parts, branchless in their efforts to grow tall.
- ☐ There are over 1000 different species of trees, including such hardwoods as mahogany, rosewood and greenheart.
- ☐ Dense undergrowth develops near rivers or forest clearings where sunlight can penetrate.

Some physical problems in developing equatorial areas.

- ☐ The high humidity encourages disease.
- ☐ The almost daily convectional storms cause considerable flooding in the Amazon lowlands.
- ☐ It is difficult and expensive to clear the forest initially, and then to keep it cleared.
- ☐ The rapid erosion and loss of fertility in the soil discourages farming (Figure 2.6).
- ☐ It is difficult to create communications both within the area and with the outside world.
- ☐ It is difficult to search for and then develop any possible mineral resources.

Savanna (tropical grasslands)

These areas are found in central parts of continents (Figure 2.1) between latitude 5° and 15° North and South of the Equator. As the graph for Cuiaba (Figure 2.1) shows –

Summers are hot, wet (although amounts tend to be unreliable) and have a high humidity.

Winters are very warm, dry and have a low humidity.

The length of the dry season increases, and the amount of rainfall decreases

(a) with distance from the equator (less convectional rainfall), and

(b) with distance from the east coast (less rain brought by the trade winds).

This climate is said to be 'transitional', because the summers (or the wet season) are similar to the equatorial areas, while the winters (or the dry season) are more like the deserts.

Using Figure 2.7 explain why

1 Temperatures are high throughout the year.

2 Temperatures are higher in summer than in winter.

3 Summers are wet and winters are dry.

Vegetation (Figure 2.8)

The dry season
The scattered deciduous trees lose their leaves, grasses turn yellow and dry up; and the ground assumes a dusty, brown-like colour. Trees shed leaves or produce thin, waxy and even thornlike leaves to try to keep transpiration to a minimum. Most trees are xerophytic (drought resistant), with very long roots to tap underground water supplies or thick bark to store water in their trunks like the baobab tree. Grasses grow tall and coarse in tufts, often separated by patches of bare soil. In this season their stalks are stiff, yellow and straw-like. Their seeds may lie dormant on the ground for the several months of drought.

The wet season
The early rains may cause soil erosion as they fall upon bare soil, but the grass seeds soon germinate, and the trees produce new leaves. Under such hot, wet conditions the grasses grow quickly and may reach a height of four metres before flowering and producing seeds. However the high temperatures reduce the effectiveness of the rainfall; the grasses are soon scorched and turn yellow and wither as the rains retreat. Rainfall totals are insufficient for many trees to grow, except near the equatorial margins.

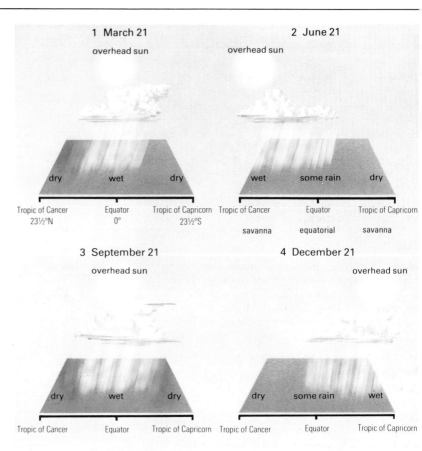

△ **Figure 2.7** Causes of seasonal rainfall patterns in a savanna climate

Problems in the savannas

- □ The long winter drought.
- □ The heavy downpours in summer, many of which cause local flooding.
- □ Soil erosion.
- □ Poor quality grass proving insufficient for the breeding of high quality cattle.

◁ **Figure 2.8** Savanna grassland, Brazil

Trade-wind coasts

These are found (Figure 2.9) on east coasts of the Americas within the tropics and facing the prevailing trade winds. This climate zone does not penetrate far inland because mountains usually rise close to the shore. The temperatures are very warm throughout the year, and the trades give high rainfall totals as they rise over the coastal mountains. The resultant vegetation is tropical rainforest, showing many of the characteristics described on page 17, together with mangrove swamps in tidal stretches.

Hurricanes

Hurricanes are severe tropical storms which bring high winds and torrential rain to the areas shown on Figure 2.9. These storms develop over the warm tropical seas, usually in autumn, and move rapidly onshore on unpredictable courses. Figure 2.10 shows a satellite photograph of a hurricane.

Weather associated with the passing of a hurricane

As the storm approaches both temperatures and pressure fall rapidly, and clouds and wind speed both increase. Increasingly longer and heavier squally showers precede a period of torrential rain accompanied by gusts of wind in excess of 160 kilometres per hour (Figure 2.11). Over 100 mm of rain can fall in an hour, and thunder and lightning is usual. Then suddenly the 'eye' passes – a period of calm when the wind and rain stops, and the sun may make a brief appearance before the full onslaught begins again and then gradually decreases as the hurricane moves on.

Consequences

☐ High winds cause considerable damage to buildings and to crops. This is catastrophic in countries which rely on one main crop, such as Nicaragua, which relies on bananas.

☐ Coastal areas suffer severe flooding resulting from high tides and storm waves, and this can cause considerable loss of life.

☐ Developing countries in Central America and the West Indies suffer most. The greatest damage occurs in countries least able to afford such a disaster.

Honduras 1974

'*Hurricane Fifi arrived at dead of night on 18 September with winds of over 200 kilometres per hour. Over half a metre of rain fell in 36 hours. Although the hurricane winds caused the initial damage, most of the estimated 8000 deaths were the result of swollen rivers sweeping away virtually everything in their paths. The poorly-built homes of the farmers – stone, wattle and clay – just disappeared. Even some of the sturdier houses were transported several miles. Those inhabitants who escaped the floods then faced another danger – cholera. Crops, for export and home use, and livestock were virtually all lost.*'

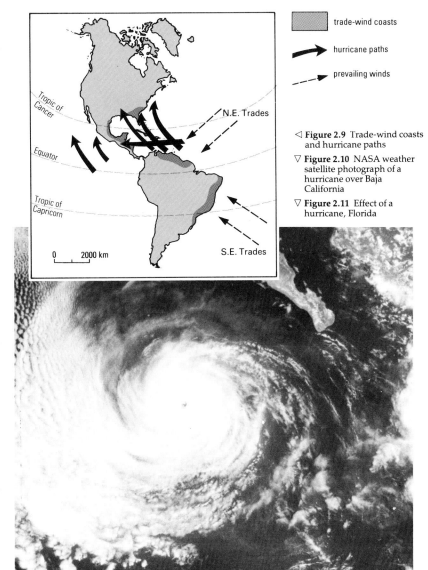

trade-wind coasts

hurricane paths

prevailing winds

◁ **Figure 2.9** Trade-wind coasts and hurricane paths

▽ **Figure 2.10** NASA weather satellite photograph of a hurricane over Baja California

▽ **Figure 2.11** Effect of a hurricane, Florida

Deserts

These areas receive less than 250 mm of rain a year, and most have high rates of evaporation. Figure 2.12 shows how much of the Americas suffer from a shortage of rain. The hot deserts of south-west America and Atacama (see Figure 2.1) suffer from:

□ High day-time (50°C) and low night-time (0°C) temperatures caused by the absence of cloud cover.

□ Unreliable and insufficient rainfall because

  (a) Air from the upper atmosphere descends near the tropics and in doing so becomes warmed and able to absorb more water vapour.

  (b) Trade winds blowing from the east will have deposited their moisture nearer the east coast.

  (c) The Rockies and Andes produce a rain-shadow effect.

  (d) There are cold offshore currents (e.g. Californian and Peruvian).

□ Soils deficient in humus and moisture.

□ A lack (though rarely a total absence) of vegetation cover (Figure 2.13).

How the vegetation is adapted to the climate

□ Seeds can germinate rapidly, and plants complete their life cycle in two or three weeks to take advantage of the occasional heavy shower (Figure 2.14).

□ Many seeds can lie dormant for several months or even years until a heavy shower occurs.

□ Plants such as the acacias have extremely long roots to tap any underground water supplies.

▷ **Figure 2.12** Location of deserts in the Americas

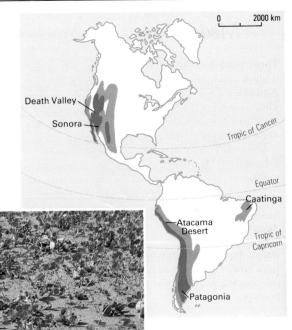

■ arid and very arid areas

■ semi-arid areas

◁ **Figure 2.14** The Atacama desert in bloom following rain

□ Plants such as cacti have thick, waxy skins to reduce transpiration, and fleshy stems which store water.

□ Many shrubs have thin, spiky or glossy leaves also to reduce transpiration (e.g. thornbush and cactus).

□ Some plants can survive in salty depressions.

▽ **Figure 2.13** Atacama desert, Chile

Development

Development of the deserts has been limited to those areas where there are oases, where water can be obtained for irrigation (e.g. lower Colorado valley), or where valuable minerals can be found (e.g. copper in northern Chile). However, despite efforts to try to develop such areas, the desert is advancing in many places.

Mediterranean areas

These warm temperate west coasts are found (Figure 2.1) in the Californian area of North America and in central Chile in South America. They lie between 30° and 40° North and South of the Equator in a narrow belt between the Rockies or Andes and the Pacific Ocean.

The climate, as shown by Valparaiso (Figure 2.1), is characterised by:

☐ Hot, dry summers.

☐ Warm, wet winters.

Indeed, it forms a transition between the hot deserts towards the Equator (and like them it receives dry offshore trade winds in summer) and the cool temperate western margins towards the pole (with their winters being both mild and moist because the prevailing winds at the time blow from the sea).

Vegetation

The vegetation has to adapt to the seasonal drought. It is mainly broad leaved evergreen forest with:

☐ Small, waxy, glossy leaves to reduce transpiration.

☐ Long tap roots to reach underground water supplies.

☐ Grass and aromatic herbs which complete their life-cycles before the onset of the drought.

☐ A slow annual growth, checked by drought in summer but permitted in winter by the mild temperatures.

California is the home of the giant Sequoia (Redwood) tree (Figure 2.15), but in drier areas (250–500 mm) or in wetter ones which have been deforested, a more stunted forest, or even

sagebrush vegetation known as 'chaparral' has developed (Figure 2.16). There has been less interference with the natural vegetation in central Chile, partly because that country developed later than other areas with a Mediterranean climate.

Problems of development

☐ The summer drought affects agriculture by retarding the growth rate of plants. The highest temperatures (and therefore evaporation rates), coincide with the time of minimum rainfall, but otherwise the high incidence of sunlight is ideal for crops and fruit.

☐ Heat and drought of summer can produce serious forest and bush fires. Several film stars living in the Hollywood/Beverly Hills suburbs of Los Angeles have lost their homes in this way.

☐ The meeting of warm air from the land and cold air from the offshore Californian and Peruvian cold sea currents causes coastal fogs which can lead to smog in an industrialised region such as Los Angeles.

☐ There are relatively large amounts of mountainous land with thin soils.

▽ **Figure 2.16** Chaparral vegetation, California

▽ **Figure 2.15** Giant Redwoods, Yosemite

Warm temperate eastern margins

This climate is also found between 30° and 40° North and South of the Equator but, unlike the Mediterranean climates, it extends up the Atlantic coasts of the south-east USA and the Pampas of Argentina-Uruguay (Figure 2.1). As the climate graph (Figure 2.1) for Buenos Aires shows, this climate is slightly warmer than the Mediterranean especially in winter because of the presence of warm offshore currents (Gulf Stream and Brazilian). The growing season is continuous throughout the year. It is also wetter than west coasts, receiving rain at all seasons, although amounts do tend to increase in summer and autumn. The reasons for this are:

- The trade winds blow onshore, having collected moisture when crossing the warm seas.
- The sun is higher in the sky and causes convectional storms.
- Autumn is the 'hurricane' season in the south-east USA (page 21).

Annual amounts tend to be greater in the south-east USA than on the Pampas, and this helps to account for the differences in natural vegetation between the two areas.

South-east USA is mixed forest, with conifers on areas of sandy soil. Little natural vegetation remains (apart from such areas as the Everglades of Florida – see Figure 2.17).

The Pampas, being almost flat, with slightly less rainfall and stronger winds, are almost devoid of trees, and the natural vegetation is tall, tussocky grass (Figure 2.18). Rainfall, and the quality of grass, decreases inland.

△ **Figure 2.17** Everglades, Florida

Problems of development

- Serious soil erosion resulting from the heavy rain (although this has mainly been in the south-east USA after the natural vegetation was cleared for crops).

- Winds: *(a)* The hurricanes of south-east USA.
  (b) The *pampero* on the Pampas, which brings cold air from the Antarctic.

▽ **Figure 2.18** Pampas grassland, Argentina

Cool temperate coasts

These are found 40° North and South of the Equator (Figure 2.1).

Western margins

Western margins climates are found in Oregon, Washington and British Columbia (North America) and in southern Chile (South America). The climate (see Valdiva, Figure 2.1) has mild winters (due to the presence of warm offshore currents) and cool summers. The annual range is small, due to the moderating influence of the sea. Frosts and snow are relatively uncommon at sea-level. However, coastal areas are limited as young

fold mountains rise inland. These mountains also force moist air brought in by westerly winds from the Pacific, in the form of depressions with their associated fronts, to rise rapidly giving heavy annual amounts of precipitation (over 3000 mm a year in southern Chile). At sea-level the natural vegetation is deciduous forest, for the winters are cold enough to limit vegetation growth and so the trees shed their leaves. However, as height above sea level increases the resultant decrease in temperatures enables such coniferous trees as the Douglas fir (Figure 2.19) to become the climax vegetation. Figure 2.20 illustrates the effect of gales on trees in south Chile.

◁ **Figure 2.19** Douglas firs on the Coast Range, California

△ **Figure 2.20** Trees contorted by the wind, Tierra del Fuego

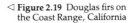

◁ **Figure 2.21** Deciduous woodland, Connecticut

Eastern margins

North-east USA, St Lawrence lowlands and the Maritime Provinces

Although still in the prevailing westerly wind belt, this time the winds blow from the land, bringing warm air in summer (New York is noted for its oppressive heat) and very cold air in winter (New York and its regions can experience severe blizzards), especially if air is drawn from the Arctic. Deciduous trees, especially the maple and beech, thrive here (Figure 2.21), but need to shed their leaves in the cold winters.

Patagonia, in Southern Argentina, is a semi-arid area, for the westerly winds have shed virtually all their moisture on crossing the Andes and warm as they descend the eastern slopes. The strength of the winds adds to the drying effect, and the resultant natural vegetation is poor quality, tussocky grass with the drought resistant cacti.

Temperate continental

This is found in the central areas of North America (the Prairies of Canada and the USA (Figure 2.1)). Nowhere in southern South America is far enough from the sea for this climate to occur.

Problems of the continental climate

☐ **Temperatures** Because there is no moderating influence of the sea, the annual range is extremely high (Saskatoon 38°C – see Figure 2.1). Central areas of continents absorb incoming radiation from the sun and heat up faster than areas near to the sea to give very warm summers. But they also lose heat rapidly in winter, when the skies are clear and the sun is at a low angle in the sky, to give extremely low temperatures (Saskatoon – see Figure 2.1) and several months of frost. The clear skies also give rise to large daily temperature ranges.

☐ **Precipitation** Amounts are light (about 500 mm a year) and decrease westwards towards the mountains. The whole region is in the rain shadow of the Rockies. Amounts are also unreliable, and droughts can occur – the worst being a succession of dry years in the 1930s which led to the 'Dust Bowl' of the Mid-West. Although there is a summer maximum of rain, this often comes as destructive convectional and hail storms. Winters give powdery snowfalls.

☐ **Blizzards** result from high winds and cold temperatures.

☐ **The Chinook** (Figure 2.23) can be an advantage to farmers, but its drying effect can cause avalanches and forest fires.

☐ **Tornadoes** (or 'twisters'). These (Figure 2.24) result from the mixing of cold arctic and warm gulf (of Mexico) air sweeping into the centre of the continent. Wind speeds in excess of 300 kilometres per hour can cause considerable loss of life and damage to property.

Vegetation

Trees can only grow along water-courses (e.g. willow), otherwise the natural vegetation is tall, prairie grasses. These lie dormant in winter, which lasts for several months under 6°C – the minimum temperature for grass growth – but grow rapidly as the temperatures rise and the snow melts in spring. As the climate turns drier to the west, the grass becomes shorter and more tussocky, and provides a less even cover. Individual blades of grass turn inwards to reduce moisture loss.

▽ **Figure 2.22** Dust storm (below left)

▽ **Figure 2.23** The Chinook

▽ **Figure 2.24** Tornado in Nebraska, this caused $50 000 worth of damage to property and was one of six tornadoes in the same day (below right)

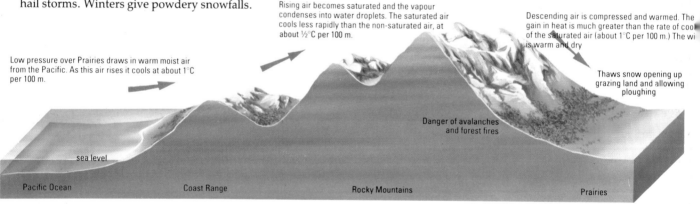

Rising air becomes saturated and the vapour condenses into water droplets. The saturated air cools less rapidly than the non-saturated air, at about ½°C per 100 m.

Descending air is compressed and warmed. The gain in heat is much greater than the rate of cool of the saturated air (about 1°C per 100 m.) The wi is warm and dry

Low pressure over Prairies draws in warm moist air from the Pacific. As this air rises it cools at about 1°C per 100 m.

Thaws snow opening up grazing land and allowing ploughing

Danger of avalanches and forest fires

sea level

Pacific Ocean

Coast Range

Rocky Mountains

Prairies

Cold climates

These (Figure 2.1) cover much of the Canadian Shield and the St Lawrence Valley as well as many higher parts of the Rockies and Andes.

Climate (Dawson City, Figure 2.1)

Winters are both very long and very cold, with the hours of sunlight very limited nearer the Arctic Circle. Summers are cool (the sun is still low in the sky) and the growing season is short although there are long hours of daylight.

Precipitation is light, being mainly snow in winter and convectional rain in summer, but amounts are not as critical to vegetation growth as are the temperatures.

Vegetation

Vegetation consists of vast stands of coniferous (Boreal) trees (Figure 2.25). The most common is the spruce, and this (Figure 2.26) like other conifers, such as the pine, fir and larch (the latter is not an evergreen) has adapted itself to the severe climatic conditions. These are the softwoods, so valuable not just for timber, but especially for the manufacture of pulp and paper. In the lower, wetter areas of the Rockies, the Douglas fir grows up to 100 metres in height. To the north the vegetation thins out into the tundra, with the trees getting increasingly more stunted in growth and more widely spaced out.

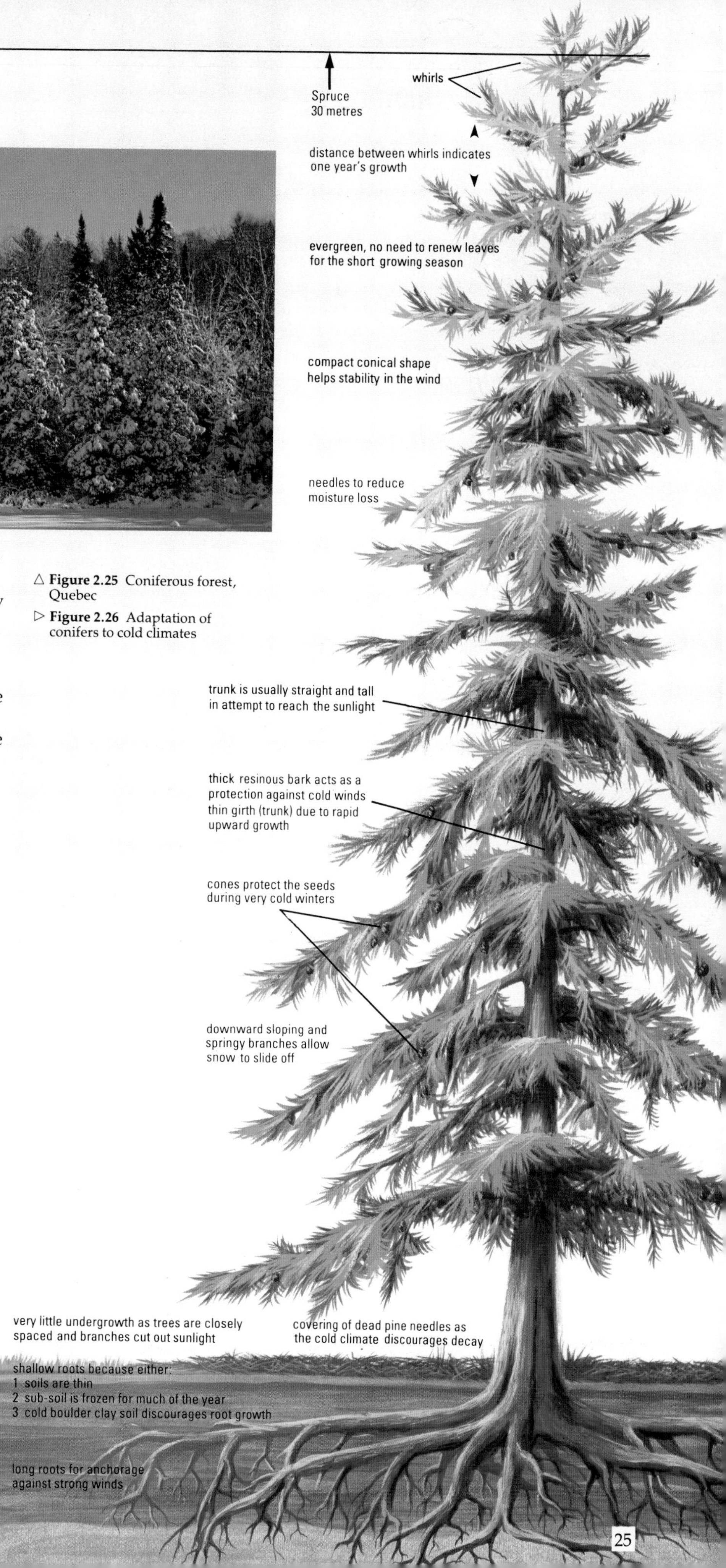

△ **Figure 2.25** Coniferous forest, Quebec

▷ **Figure 2.26** Adaptation of conifers to cold climates

Spruce
30 metres

whirls

distance between whirls indicates one year's growth

evergreen, no need to renew leaves for the short growing season

compact conical shape helps stability in the wind

needles to reduce moisture loss

trunk is usually straight and tall in attempt to reach the sunlight

thick resinous bark acts as a protection against cold winds thin girth (trunk) due to rapid upward growth

cones protect the seeds during very cold winters

downward sloping and springy branches allow snow to slide off

very little undergrowth as trees are closely spaced and branches cut out sunlight

covering of dead pine needles as the cold climate discourages decay

shallow roots because either:
1 soils are thin
2 sub-soil is frozen for much of the year
3 cold boulder clay soil discourages root growth

layer of peat over clay

long roots for anchorage against strong winds

Arctic climates

These occur in the extreme north of Canada and Alaska (Figure 2.1). The graph for Barrow (Figure 2.1) shows some of the climatic problems of this region.

☐ Winters are extremely long and cold, and air temperatures can fall to −40°C. For several weeks the sun never rises.

☐ The wind-chill factor is high. This is the result of strong winds which evaporate moisture, freeze the skin and cause frost-bite.

☐ Blizzards result from strong winds blowing the dry, powdery snow.

☐ The long, continuous frosts of the northern area cause the ground to be permanently frozen – the so-called permafrost. This (Figure 2.27) can be over 300 metres deep.

☐ The more southern areas have up to four months above freezing point, and with the sun low in the sky often for several weeks, the surface melts, forming the active layer (Figure 2.27). Because of the frozen subsoil, the low rates of evaporation and the gentle relief, much of the surface becomes waterlogged (Figure 2.28).

△ **Figure 2.28** The tundra in summer in the Canadian Arctic. The frozen subsoil causes the melting snow to stand as pools of water on the surface of the ground

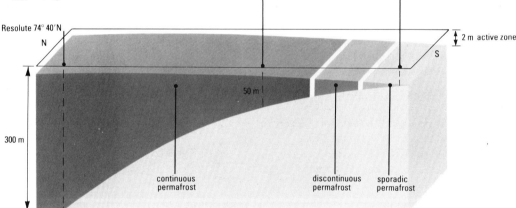

▷ **Figure 2.27** A cross-section showing how permafrost decreases from north to south

Vegetation

This area is known as the tundra ('tree-less plain'). The growth of tundra vegetation is seriously affected by the permafrost, for even where the snow does melt, roots cannot penetrate into the frozen ground. Plants must adapt to a short life cycle, to the thin active layer (for which they need short roots) and to finding shelter against the biting winds (for which they must be low-growing). On south facing, sheltered, drier slopes carpets of brightly coloured flowers called 'bloom-mats' grow (Figure 2.29), together with such berry-bearing plants as the bilberry. In the more poorly drained areas mosses predominate, and the numerous exposed rocks are covered in lichens. Nearer to rivers, stunted willow and birch struggle for survival.

▷ **Figure 2.29** Brightly coloured 'bloom-mats' grow in the short summer on the tundra

Mountain climates

As was seen in Chapter One, high mountain ranges extend from Alaska in the north to Tierra del Fuego in the south. The highest peaks in both North and South America exceed 6000 metres. The difference in altitude, often abrupt, causes rapid modification in climate.

Characteristics

☐ **Temperatures** As the air is thin and clear it has little ability to absorb heat from the sun. Temperatures decrease, on average, by 1°C for every 150 metres of height. This means that even in Ecuador on the Equator, while day-time temperatures at Guayaquil on the coast may be over 30°C, at about 6000 metres on top of such volcanoes as Cotopaxi and Chimborazo, the temperature will be only −10°C, hence the permanent snow cover. In winter days may be sunny but the incoming energy is reflected by the snow. The snow-line is the lowest level of permanent snow cover.

☐ **Precipitation** Where moist, warm air is forced to rise by mountains, it is cooled until the vapour is condensed into clouds and rain or, where temperatures are low enough, into snow. The windward sides may receive high amounts of precipitation while the sheltered leeward slopes are in a rain-shadow. Heavy rains also wash away any accumulations of soil.

☐ **Winds** These also can be strong, and windward slopes suffer from exposure giving less vegetation cover than on the sheltered leeward side.

☐ **Pressure** The decrease in pressure and oxygen can cause mountain sickness to humans.

Vegetation

Vegetation is also modified by height. Figure 2.30 shows the altitudinal changes in the latitudes of California, and Figure 2.31 shows the vegetation zones of the Andes. The tree-line (the maximum height at which trees grow) decreases poleward from 4500 metres on the equator to 2000 metres at 40°N and S, and to sea-level on the Arctic Circle.

▽ **Figure 2.30** Altitudinal changes in vegetation in North America

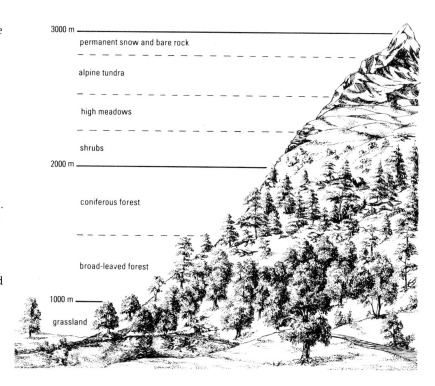

3000 m — permanent snow and bare rock

alpine tundra

high meadows

shrubs

2000 m — coniferous forest

broad-leaved forest

1000 m — grassland

▽ **Figure 2.31** Vegetation zones across the Andes (at about 16°S)

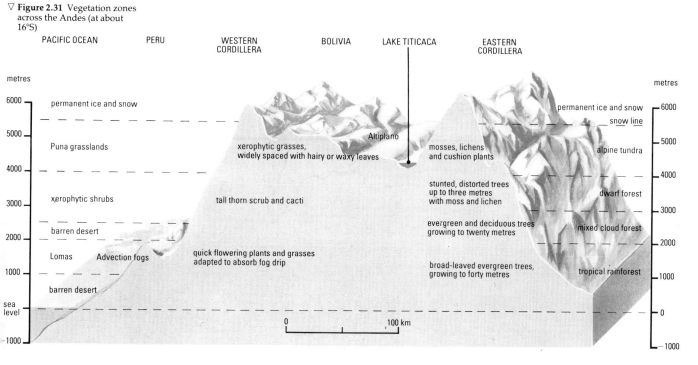

Origins

Distributions and movements

A race is a group of people having their own inherited characteristics distinguishing them from peoples of other races. In reality, often because of later intermarriages, the border line between different races is indistinct; there may be a wide range in the characteristics of the members of a race, and even of a family or tribe in that race. It is generally accepted that there are three main races. The distinctive characteristics of these three are given in Figure 3.1, their location and source of origin in the Americas is shown in Figure 3.2, and their appearances in Figure 3.3.

Races live together, particularly in areas of high population density, and this can lead to:

☐ Racial integration, as is usual in Brazil, or

☐ Racial tension, as between 'whites' and 'blacks' in parts of the south-east of the USA.

▷ **Figure 3.2** Origins of racial groups in the Americas

▷ **Figure 3.3** Different racial groups in the Americas today

Caucasoid
(originating in the Caucasus)

Anglo-Americans
(from NW Europe especially Britain)

Latin Americans
(from Spain and Portugal)

---

1 Are there separate races?

It is possible to divide the world's population into three broad groups based on physical differences to do with skin and hair colour. Figure 3.3 shows how this division can be applied to groups in North and South America.

2 What are the shortcomings of this view?

a) Groups of people differ from one another in language, place of birth, religion, the traditions they develop, and so on. These differences mean that there are many ethnic groups, not three racial groups.

b) Think of a photograph to go under the label 'Latin Americans' in Figure 3.3. This group would not regard itself as belonging to the same ethnic group as the Anglo-American in the first photograph.

c) In recent years, people from Africa, the Caribbean and parts of Asia have preferred to be known collectively as black. The aim of this is to identify a group with a common experience both past and present. What is the common experience linking the Eskimo with the Negro from the south of North America?

 Negroid

Caucasoid

Mongoloid (Amerin

 Mongoloid (Asiatics

△ **Figure 3.1** Racial characteristics

▽ **Figure 3.4** Inhabitants of the Americas in A.D. 1492, the year Columbus landed in the West Indies

▽ **Figure 3.5** Origins of racial groups in the Americas, 1980s

From 20,000 to 15,000 B.C. there were mongoloid migrations via the land bridge between Asia and Alaska when the sea level was lower that it is today

Eskimos

Red Indians

Tropic of Cancer

Aztecs

Equator

Lowland Indians

Incas

Tropic of Capricorn

0   2000 km

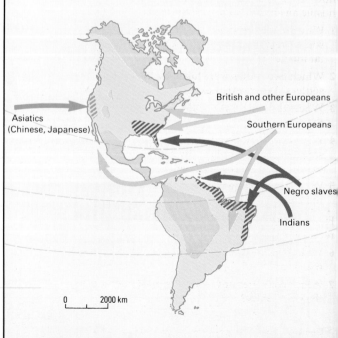

Asiatics (Chinese, Japanese)

British and other Europeans

Southern Europeans

Negro slaves

Indians

0   2000 km

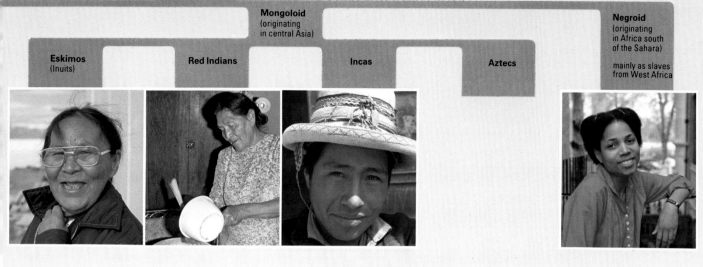

Homo Sapiens

Mongoloid (originating in central Asia)

Negroid (originating in Africa south of the Sahara) mainly as slaves from West Africa

Eskimos (Inuits)

Red Indians

Incas

Aztecs

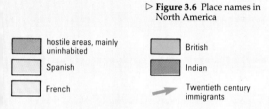

▷ **Figure 3.6** Place names in North America

- hostile areas, mainly uninhabited
- Spanish
- French
- British
- Indian
- → Twentieth century immigrants

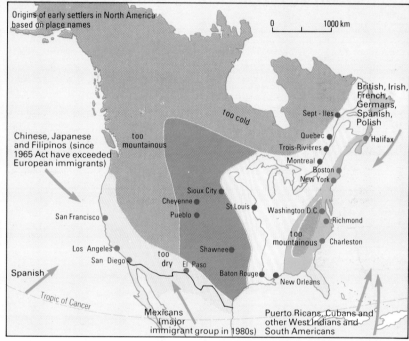

Origins of early settlers in North America based on place names

0   1000 km

too cold

too mountainous

Chinese, Japanese and Filipinos (since 1965 Act have exceeded European immigrants)

Sept - Iles

British, Irish, French, Germans, Spanish, Polish

Quebec

Halifax

Trois-Rivières

Montreal

Boston

New York

Sioux City

Cheyenne

St Louis

Washington D.C.

Pueblo

Richmond

San Francisco

too mountainous

Charleston

Los Angeles

Shawnee

San Diego

too dry

El Paso

Spanish

Baton Rouge

New Orleans

Tropic of Cancer

Mexicans (major immigrant group in 1980s)

Puerto Ricans, Cubans and other West Indians and South Americans

Migrations into North America

When Europeans first landed in the Americas, all the native Americans were derived from the Mongoloid race (Figure 3.4), yet today these people have been pushed by 'colonists' into areas which are both isolated and lacking in resources (Figure 3.5).

If you look at North American place names in an atlas (or Figure 3.6), it is possible to tell from which European country the early 'settlers' came. Notice how several parts of the continent proved to be too hostile an environment to settle in.

1 Why do you think that the Spanish settled in the south-west? And why did they not push very far inland?

2 Which two routes were taken by the French settlers? Why were these good routes to follow?

3 Where did the British settle? Why did they settle there?

4 What do you notice about the location of Indian-sounding settlements? Why are they not evenly distributed over the continent?

5 Why were Negroes taken to the south-east of the USA?

Figure 3.6 and especially Figure 3.7 show more recent migration into the USA.

6 Which countries now send fewer migrants to the USA? Why?

7 Which countries now send the most migrants to the USA? Why?

▷ **Figure 3.7** Recent changes in the sources of United States immigrants (by country of birth)

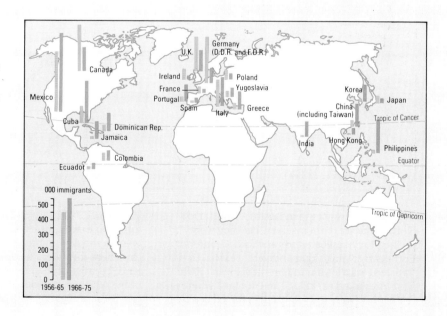

Canada

U.K.

Germany (D.D.R. and F.D.R.)

Ireland

Poland

France

Yugoslavia

Korea

Mexico

Portugal

Spain

Italy

Greece

Japan

China (including Taiwan)

Tropic of Cancer

Cuba

Dominican Rep.

Jamaica

India

Hong Kong

Philippines

Colombia

Equator

Ecuador

000 immigrants

500

400

300

200

100

0

1956-65   1966-75

Tropic of Capricorn

Minorities – North America

Canada and the USA are two very rich countries where most people are considered to have a high standard of living, large houses complete with numerous electrical gadgets, large gardens and at least two cars. Yet as in other countries of the world, there is an unequal distribution of wealth, and many North Americans are very poor. These include:

☐ Descendants of the original Amerindian (Mongoloid) tribes, e.g. Indians, Eskimos (Inuit).

☐ Descendants of former immigrants (e.g. Negroes) or present-day immigrants (e.g. Puerto Ricans).

Eskimos still live in the extreme north (Figure 3.5) but their way of life has changed drastically in the last two or three decades (Figure 3.8).

Recent movements are now away from trying to integrate Eskimos into the North American way of life and attempting to give them some self-determination, yet their lives have not necessarily improved. They have to use textbooks in English and have been forced to give up their traditional way of life. To others in the continent they are regarded as lazy because they rely upon welfare payments, yet in reality they do not possess the education or the skills for present-day jobs – that is assuming they can find jobs in the Arctic areas.

	Traditional way of life (pre 1960)	present day way of life
settlements	nomadic	small permanent settlements
houses	igloos in winter, tents in summer	pre-fabricated, oil heated buildings
transport	huskies with sledge, kayaks	snowmobiles, local airstrip
food	hunting caribou, and fishing in summer; hunting seal and polar bear in winter; hunting up to 10 bowhead whales each spring	international agreement limits number of whales caught to two per year; much food imported (by air)
clothes	furs	furs and western style clothes
social amenities	none	usually a shop, school, medical centre, village hall, electricity, TV, water supply, sewage
occupations	mainly hunting and fishing for themselves	fishing (char sells well in Canada), social services, some tourism, and (in Alaska) oil

Figure 3.8 Changes in the Eskimo way of life (above left)

◁ **Figure 3.9** Indian reservations in the USA, 1875 and 1980

 Indian reservations 198

 Indian reservations 187

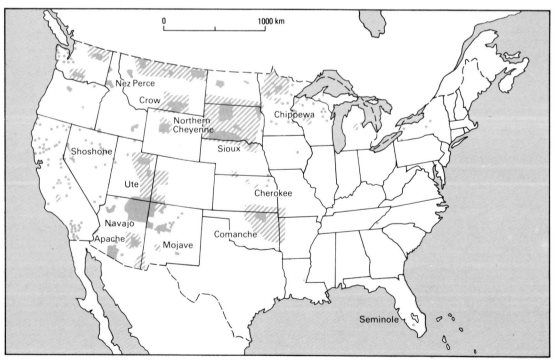

Indians Until 1492 the Indian tribes had all of North America to themselves, but they were pushed further westwards and into the interior as European colonists demanded more land. In 'Western' movies the Indians have been totally misrepresented as 'killers' and 'looters' whereas in reality they were only fighting to try to keep their land. By 1875 (Figure 3.9) the Indians had been forced to live on reservations, 75 per cent of which were in the dry, mountainous western states. Yet even here they were forced to 'sell' and 'concede' land, because of their own poverty and the needs of the white man to develop new mineral resources and even to create national parks.

△ **Figure 3.10** Pueblo Indian Reservation (San Geronimo in New Mexico)

Percentage of blacks in total population, 1970	
▨	over 50
▧	20 to 50
▨	5 to 19
▨	under 5

Black populations in cities (thousands)	
○	100 to 199
○	200 to 399
○	400 to 599
○	600 to 999
○	1000 to 1668

The figures for the larger cities show the black percentage of total population

▽ **Figure 3.11** Distribution of Negroes in the USA

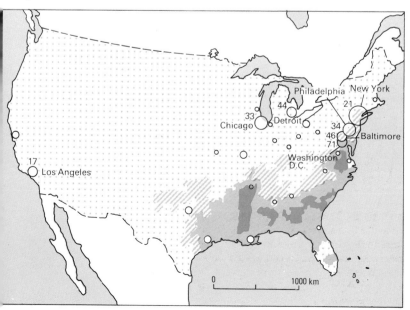

Present-day problems include:

□ Low standard of living – on average in 1982 56 per cent below that of white families.

□ A high birth rate, an infant mortality rate above the national average and a population growth rate three times greater than the national average.

□ Higher incidence of disease and a shorter expectancy of life than the whites.

□ High unemployment, partly due to their having to live in isolated areas of poor quality farmland which lack natural resources. The Navajo Indians have over 80 per cent unemployment compared to the national average of 10 per cent. The result is a drift to the towns and a reliance upon welfare payments.

□ 90 per cent live in substandard housing (Figure 3.10).

□ Limited schooling leaves many illiterate and lacking in technical skills.

□ There is a high rate of alcoholism, violent crime and malnutrition. Alcohol is now banned on most reservations, so the addicted move to larger cities.

The **Navajo Indians** (Figure 3.9) form the largest group of Indians. They live east of the Grand Canyon and try to earn a living by rearing sheep on semi-desert type vegetation, and making blankets and silver ornaments for tourists. Since 1972 they have been given control of their reservations, but they remain a highly deprived minority group in the USA.

Negroes They were brought originally to North America as slaves. They are now (Figure 3.11) concentrated especially:

□ In the south-east of the USA (the former cotton belt) where they were used on plantations.

□ In the large cities of the north and east such as Washington D.C., Baltimore, Detroit, Chicago and New York.

□ In inner city areas (as in Britain) in ghettos such as Harlem in New York (page 45).

Despite some improvements since the civil rights movement of the 1960s, the Negroes remain socially and economically 'deprived' in comparison to the whites, and their position has weakened as the recession of the 1980s increases.

Percentage below the poverty line in the USA

	1959	1982
Whites	11.0	9.2
Non-whites	28.5	30.8

Illegal immigrants from Mexico are the USA's latest problem. Originally many came to California for seasonal fruit and vegetable picking but now many try to stay or to move illegally across the border, for they are conscious of the higher standard of life and better job opportunities in the USA.

Groupings in Latin America

Figure 3.12 shows the multi-racial make-up of people living in South and Central America today.

☐ **Amerindians** are the descendants of the original Mongoloid settlers.

Highland Indians live in Mexico, Central America and the Andean states.

Lowland Indians live in the Amazon Basin and Central America.

☐ **Negroes** live in the Caribbean Islands and the coastal areas of Brazil. They are descendants of African slaves.

☐ **Europeans** tend to have settled in cooler areas of the continent. They form higher percentages in Argentina and Chile.

☐ **Mestizos** are numerous throughout the continent. They result from mixed marriages, especially between Europeans (Spanish and Portuguese) and Amerindians.

☐ **Asians** have become the latest group of immigrants to the area, moving into both the Caribbean and Brazil. Brazil now contains the largest Japanese community outside Japan.

Figure 3.13 shows the multiracial composition of the Brazilian football team. Indeed it is difficult to try to determine from which race each player actually originated.

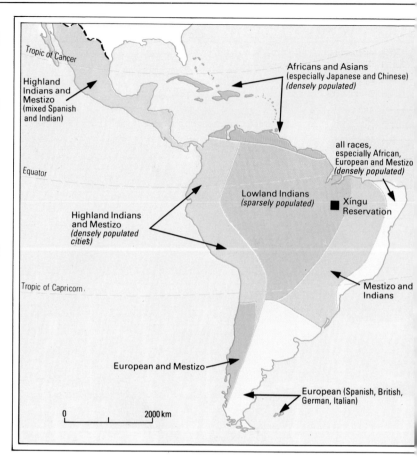

△ **Figure 3.12** Racial groups in Latin America

The Lowland Indians

Amerindians of the Amazon Basin

These have, over the centuries, adapted to the harsh life of the equatorial rain forests.

☐ Houses and furniture come from the forest trees, the thatch from the leaves, and all are held together by the lianas.

▽ **Figure 3.13** Brazil's 1982 World Cup football team

Amerindians
(Mongoloid)

Europeans
(Caucasoid)

Africans (Negroid)
and Asians
(Mongoloid)

Mestizo (mixed
marriages)
and Amerindian

European and
Mestizo

extremely mixed

△ **Figure 3.14** Member of the Megkronotis tribe in his black war paint

- Pottery comes from clay from river beds.
- Food comes from *hunting* animals (wild pig, monkey), *fishing, collecting* (fruits, berries) and *growing crops* (manioc, maize and yams).
- Farming is the 'slash and burn' type (Chapter 6), where a small section of forest is temporarily cleared and is farmed for up to five years.

Recent developments in the Amazon Basin

- The Trans-Amazonica Highway and other roads (Chapter 13).
- General deforestation for timber (Chapter 9).
- Vast deforestation for cattle ranches. By 1980 over six million cattle were being reared in former forested areas.
- Development of mines and sawmills.
- Decimation of the Amerindian population, due partly to massacres at the hands of new settlers from the east coast and partly to deaths from disease brought in by the settlers, against which the Indians had no immunity. An original population of about 4 million is now down to 120 000.

The Xingu Reservation

This was created in 1961 in the Xingu Valley (see Figure 3.12) for 14 tribes, including the Megkronotis with its chief, Raoni. These tribes are seen by the white man as both a nuisance to any development scheme such as clearing the forest for roads and ranches, and as killers of the developers. Progress cannot be halted. But to

these Megkronotis it is a fight for their land and their lives. The woodcutters even in the 1970s were clearing the forest with bulldozers and fire at the rate of 100 hectares a day. Game and fish supplies were dwindling fast. Raoni tried to negotiate with an ineffectual government department run for Indian affairs, but progress was slow, for the limits to the reservation had never been clearly drawn. In 1976 Raoni warned the woodcutters not to move any further into land traditionally belonging to the Indians, and now belonging to them by the 1961 law, unless they were prepared to face death at the hands of the tribesmen. His appeal was ignored, and more forest was burnt. Raoni's warriors put on their black war paint, took their bows, clubs and guns and set off for the woodcutters's camp with instructions to hit the workers hard enough to frighten them and to make them run away. But one Indian had had a cousin recently killed by a white man, and he hit too hard. The Indians then 'killed the rest to put them out of their misery'. Later a ferry boat across the Xingu was sunk, a bridge to bring new settlers into the Amazon was destroyed, and more white settlers were killed. Later a government officer said an agreement had been reached warning the woodcutters not to set foot on Indian land – but the woodcutters and farmers disagree and have threatened to create their own police force and to kill any Indian on 'their' land.

Should the Indians fight for their land, even if they have to kill? Or should 'progress' be allowed to take place?

Growth rates

The annual growth rate of the world's population rose slowly but steadily until the beginning of the nineteenth century, after which it has grown at an increasingly faster rate. The annual growth rate is the difference between the birth rate (i.e. the average number of births per 1000 people) and the death rate (i.e. the average number of deaths per 1000 people). Based upon growth rates in Western Europe and North America, a model has been produced (Figure 4.1) suggesting that the population (or demographic) growth rate can be divided into four distinct stages – the so-called 'population cycle'. This population cycle has also been applied to developing countries despite the fact that the model assumes that the falling death rate in stage 2 is a response to increased industrialisation, whereas many of the developing countries have undergone, as yet, only minimal industrialisation. Figure 4.1 also shows how selected American countries fit into the population cycle. Figure 4.2 illustrates why the developing countries are increasing their population at a much faster rate than the developed countries (see also Figure 4.3).

Developing countries in Latin America have:

☐ High birth rates, especially in Catholic countries. People believe that children are more important than material possessions and, in many areas, children are a symbol of a man's wealth and strength.

☐ Falling death rates, due to: increased vaccination against diseases (e.g. smallpox and polio); eradication of pests (e.g. the mosquito); an improvement in medical facilities, sanitation and personal hygiene; and an improvement in the amount of food available and a more balanced diet. Figure 4.5 shows the population increase to be about 3 per cent per year.

Developed countries in North America (Figure 4.2) have:

☐ Low death rates due to first class medical care and drugs, a high income per person to afford doctors and drugs, and a high agricultural output giving a good healthy diet (see Chapter 6).

☐ Low birth rates due to family planning, a desire for material possessions rather than too many children, and improved education and literacy.

Figure 4.5 shows the population increase in these countries to be about 1 per cent per year.

In all parts of the world, population has increased as the expectancy of life has increased. Life expectancy is the number of years that the average person born in a particular country can expect to live. Three examples of this dramatic increase in Latin America are given in Figure 4.3.

The results of these changes in birth rates, death rates and life expectancy in North and Latin America are shown in Figure 4.4. North America's high increase between 1700 and 1850 was mainly due to a high level of immigration (both voluntary and as slaves). In contrast it is Latin America which is now growing the faster, partly due to high birth rates, falling death rates, a high level of immigration and, judged by developed countries' standards, very large families.

Birth rates, death rates, life expectancy and other population figures for each country in the Americas are given in Figure 17.1 (page 124).

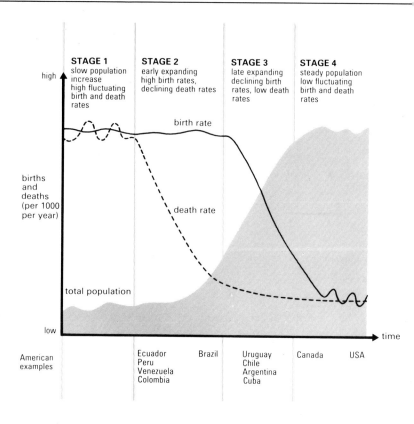

Developing countries (e.g. in South and Central America)

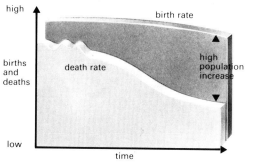

Developed countries (e.g. Canada and USA)

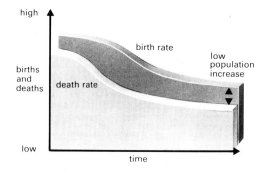

△ **Figure 4.1** The population cycle

◁ **Figure 4.2** Population grow in the Americas

▽ **Figure 4.3** The increase in li expectancy in Latin America

	Brazil	Guatemala	Mexico
1900	29	24	25
1940	37	30	39
1980	64	58	65

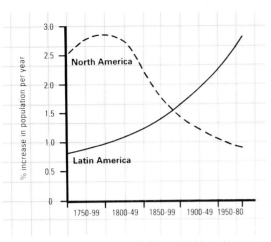

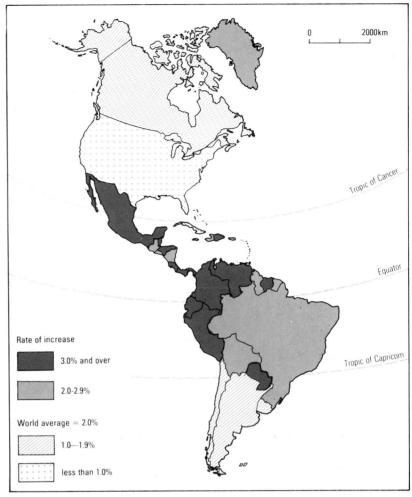

△ **Figure 4.4** Contrasts in population growth between North and Latin America

▷ **Figure 4.5** Natural increase in population

World population trends

After the growing concern expressed at the increasingly faster growth of the world's population during the 1960s and 1970s, a United Nations report entitled *The State of World Populations 1982* stated that at least the rate of growth was becoming slower. This means that the world population may reach only 6.1 billion by A.D. 2000, instead of the 7.6 billion it would have reached if the rates of growth of the period 1950–1980 had continued.

The report links the decline in birth rates to a variety of factors, including improved education, better employment opportunities and in general to rising living standards – all of which are related to a spread of family planning. After the alarmist predictions of the 1960s the report seems good news, but there are many important variations suggesting that some regions will take longer to stabilize than others.

Europe is expected to be the first region to reach zero growth. By 2030 it is likely to have added only 50 million to its present population. Its birth rate is

one of the lowest in the world at around 14 per 1,000 inhabitants. Next to level out will be North America (16.3 per 1,000) with an eventual population of 320 million.

Latin America is expected to treble its present 400 million, with the population of Mexico approaching that of the United States by 2110.

Rate of increase
- 3.0% and over
- 2.0-2.9%

World average = 2.0%
- 1.0—1.9%
- less than 1.0%

net addition to world population at 25 year intervals

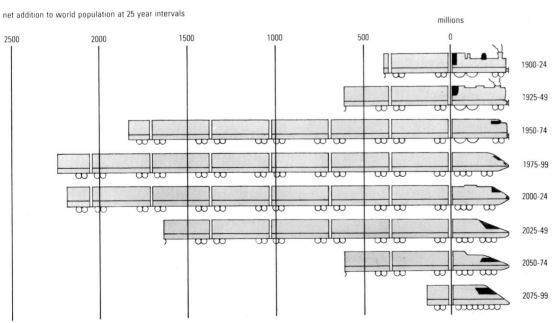

◁ **Figure 4.6** The growth of the world's population shows signs of slowing down

Population structure

The rate of natural increase, birth rate, death rate and life expectancy have a profound effect upon the population structure of a country. The division of the population into age groups is shown by an age-sex pyramid (Figure 4.7) in which the percentage of males in each group is shown on the left-hand side of the graph, and the percentage of females on the right-hand side. This method allows a comparison between countries. Figure 4.7 shows three American countries at different stages in the population cycle (Figure 4.1).

- **Peru,** like all other developing countries, has a pyramid with a broad base and a narrow peak indicating a very large number of children and very few old people. This indicates a youthful population (see also Figure 4.9) which will soon increase the numbers who enter the reproductive period and become economically active (an energetic labour force). The population growth will be rapid. It also suggests that despite the high birth rate, the infant mortality rate (the number of children who die before they are one year old) is high and the expectancy of life is relatively short.

- **Argentina** is similar to Peru in that its population indicates a high birth rate, a declining death rate and a rapidly expanding population. However, the slightly larger number of people in the economically active group suggests improving medical facilities, and more people living longer.

- **The USA** has a relatively large proportion of its population in the pre- and post-reproductive age groups, and a smaller proportion in the group capable of producing most children and national wealth. This suggests a declining population, possibly due to a period when the death rate declined dramatically or when there were fewer births.

In contrast the United Kingdom (Figure 4.8) has a 'narrow' pyramid, where numbers in each group are approximately equal. The 'dependency age' groups are large in relation to those in the economically active and reproductive sections. This represents a country with no significant population growth and an ageing population, as well as a low infant mortality rate and a high standard of medical care. In the UK, it shows that more females than males live to over 70.

The Dependency Ratio is

$$\frac{\text{the non-economically active}}{\text{economically active}}$$

i.e. $\dfrac{\text{children} + \text{elderly}}{\text{those of working age}}$

How does this ratio affect (a) the working population (b) the gross national product of a country (c) the planning and cost of social services such as hospitals, old people's homes, schools and nurseries?

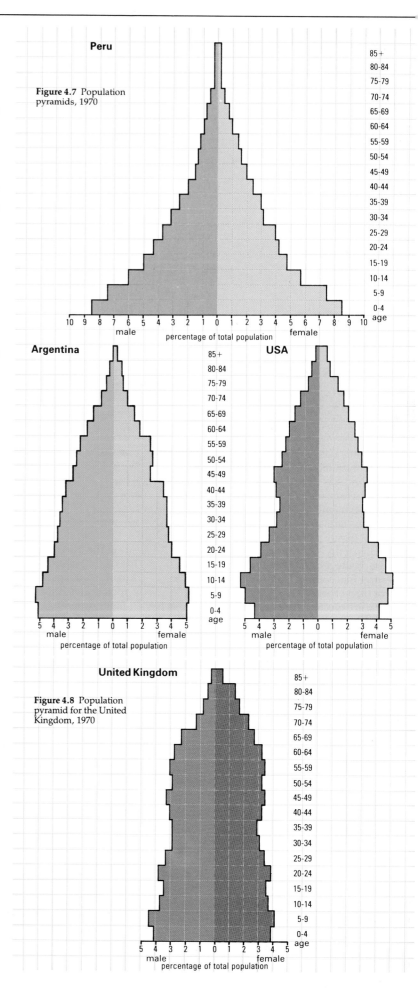

Figure 4.7 Population pyramids, 1970

Figure 4.8 Population pyramid for the United Kingdom, 1970

The increase in the world's population of under fifteen-year-olds

'Families with children into the double figures are very common in north-east Brazil. Rural mothers in this state, Rio Grande do Norte, have an average of more than seven living children. A quarter of them have ten or more. And that is not counting the dead ones. You often meet women like Luisa Gomez, a slight, small, thirty-nine-year-old. She married at fourteen. Since then she has been pregnant sixteen times, one every eighteen months. For half her adult life she has been pregnant, and for the other half breast-feeding the most recent addition. Only six of those sixteen are still alive. There were three stillbirths and seven died in their first year. Ten wasted pregnancies. Seven and a half years of drain on an already weak organism for nothing. Worse than nothing, for all the anxiety, all the care, all the concern, and then the grief.'

Figure 4.9 shows those parts of North and Latin America where the growth of the under fifteen-year-olds is greatest, and Figure 4.10 the differences in attitude to having children between Latin America (the developing world) and North America (the developed world).

% of population under 15 years

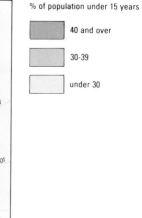

40 and over

30-39

under 30

△ **Figure 4.9** Percentage of population under fifteen years old, 1980

HOW MANY CHILDREN SHALL WE HAVE?

Developing world

average number of children per family — about five

Developed world

average number of children per family — about two

◁ **Figure 4.10** Attitude towards children in the developing and developed world.

▽ **Figure 4.11** The ageing world

The increase in the world's population of over sixty-year-olds

Because of better medical facilities, hygiene, vaccines, etc., life expectancy has increased considerably (Figure 4.3). However this does mean that there are many more elderly people who need to be looked after (Figure 4.11).

North America had a 23 per cent increase in people over 60 between 1970 and 1980. At General Motors in 1967 there were 10 present-day workers to every company pensioner. By 1980 this had fallen to 4 workers per pensioner, and by 1990 it is expected to be only 1 worker per pensioner.

Latin America had a 38 per cent increase in people over 60 between 1970 and 1980, and has less money to deal with the problems of an ageing population.

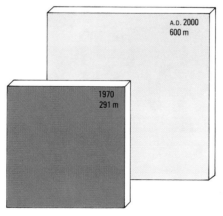

Over 60's

World age boom

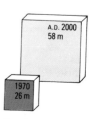

Over 80's

37

Population movement

Rural depopulation

One of the major problems facing almost all the countries in the world, and especially those in the developing world, is that of rural depopulation, i.e. the drift (or in many cases the rush) from the countryside to the towns and cities. What causes this movement?

'Push' factors (why people leave the countryside)

☐ Pressure on the land, e.g. division of land among sons, which means that each has too little to live on.

☐ Overpopulation, resulting from high birth rates, adds to the numbers which the rural area has to support.

☐ Starvation, resulting from either too little output for the people of the area, or from crop failure.

☐ Mechanisation of land (more likely in North America) has caused a reduction in jobs available on the land together with, in many areas, reduced yields.

☐ Farming is hard work with long hours and little pay. In developing countries a lack of money means a lack of machinery (Figure 4.12), pesticides and fertilisers.

☐ Natural disasters such as drought (north-east Brazil), hurricanes (West Indies), floods, volcanic eruptions and mud avalanches (Peru) destroy villages and crops.

☐ Extreme physical conditions such as aridity, rugged mountains, cold, heat, and dense vegetation.

☐ Local communities (Amazon Amerindians) forced to move.

☐ Lack of services (schools, hospitals).

▽ **Figure 4.12** Steep hillsides in Bolivia must be terraced to increase the amount of land available to support the rural population

'Pull' factors (why people move to the city)

☐ They are looking for a better paid job. Factory workers get about three times the wages of farm workers.

☐ They expect to be housed more comfortably.

☐ They expect a higher quality of life

☐ They have a better chance of such services as schools, medical treatment and entertainment.

☐ They will be nearer more reliable sources of food.

☐ Religious and political activities can be carried on more safely in larger cities.

Growth of cities (see also Chapter 5). It is estimated that throughout the world 750 000 people a day are leaving rural areas to live in cities. In Brazil the urban population has doubled in 40 years:

   1950   35% of the country's population

   1965   45% of the country's population

   1980   78% of the country's population

Seventy per cent of this urban increase has resulted from people migrating from rural areas.

Half of the inhabitants in Latin America now live in cities, and the United Nations forecasts that the next serious problem looming over the world will be how to cope with these cities. Mexico City, with a population of 13 million in 1980, is expected to reach 31 million by A.D. 2000. Sao Paulo (Figure 4.13) is expected to be almost as large. (How many people per year, then, are expected to settle in Mexico City between 1980 and A.D. 2000?)

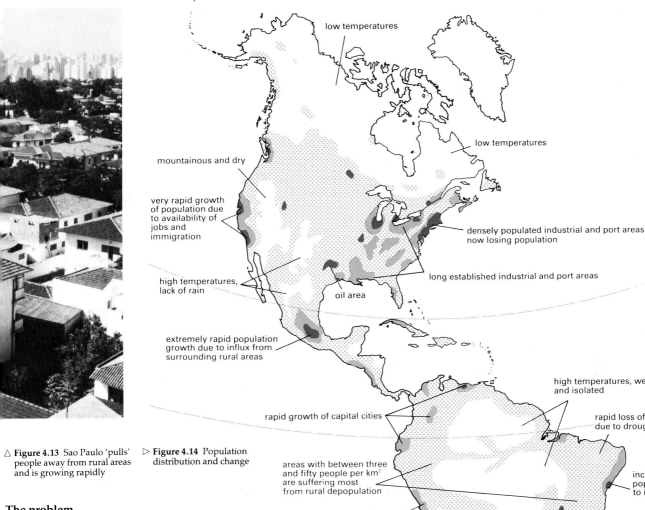

The labels on the map (Figure 4.14) read:

low temperatures

low temperatures

mountainous and dry

very rapid growth of population due to availability of jobs and immigration

densely populated industrial and port areas now losing population

high temperatures, lack of rain

long established industrial and port areas

oil area

extremely rapid population growth due to influx from surrounding rural areas

high temperatures, wet, forested and isolated

rapid growth of capital cities

rapid loss of population due to drought

areas with between three and fifty people per km² are suffering most from rural depopulation

increase in population due to immigration

rapid growth of capital cities

high temperatures, lack of rain

extremely rapid population and industrial growth

mountainous

industrial and intensive farming region

mountainous, dry and cold

0   2000km

inhabitants per km²

- over 200
- 50-200
- 3-49
- less than 3

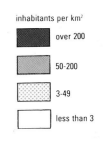

△ **Figure 4.13** Sao Paulo 'pulls' people away from rural areas and is growing rapidly

▷ **Figure 4.14** Population distribution and change

The problem

'*Trucks loaded with poor peasant immigrants came down night after night from the north-east of Brazil, two weeks' journey away. Men, women and babies travelled in open trucks, sitting on planks lashed across the truck, with the family's possessions tied up in a blanket at their feet. They called them 'parrot perch' trucks. The trucks dumped the homeless families and set off north for another load.*'

What faces these migrants when they reach the city and what problems confront the urban authorities will be described in Chapter Five.

Population density and change

Using Figure 4.14 and your knowledge, answer these questions:

1 Which densely populated area is now beginning to lose population? Why is this so?

2 Which are the three most rapidly growing areas in terms of population? Why are they growing so rapidly?

3 Which areas are suffering most from rural depopulation? Give reasons for your answer.

4 What reasons are given on the map to explain why several parts of North and Latin America have fewer than three people per km² living there?

Overpopulation

Several areas in the Americas suffer from overpopulation, but they are not necessarily the areas which have the highest density of population. The north-east of Brazil is said to be overpopulated, yet it has fewer than two people per km². This is because, although there is sufficient room for them, there is insufficient water and therefore food for the inhabitants. On the other hand, parts of California have over 500 people per km², yet they are not regarded as being overpopulated because there are sufficient jobs, houses, resources and food for their inhabitants.

Urban growth

In 1960 one-third of the world's population (3000 million) lived in urban areas. By A.D. 2000 the world's population will have doubled, and half will be living in large cities.

In 1982, 24 world cities contained over 4 million inhabitants (Figure 5.1 shows that 10 of these are in the Americas), and this is expected to exceed 60 cities worldwide by A.D. 2000. Figure 5.1 also shows the distribution of 'millionaire cities' in the Americas.

Figure 5.2 shows the rank order of the world's largest twelve cities over a period of years. In 1970 half of these were still in the industrialised, developed continents of North America and Europe. By 1985 no city in Europe is expected to be in the top twelve, whereas estimates suggest that by A.D. 2000 the two largest cities will be in Latin America (Figure 5.1 also shows that the three fastest growing cities in the world are also in Latin America), and the top eleven will all be in the developing continents of Latin America and Asia. This would confirm the present tendency of:

☐ cities within the tropics to be growing faster than cities in the temperate latitudes, and

☐ the largest city in most developing countries to be growing much faster than any other city in that country.

Both Sao Paulo and Mexico City are growing by an estimated half a million people a year – can you imagine *all* the inhabitants of Leeds or Sheffield suddenly arriving in Sao Paulo or Mexico City within a year? Think of the problems that it must pose to both the newcomers and the city authorities.

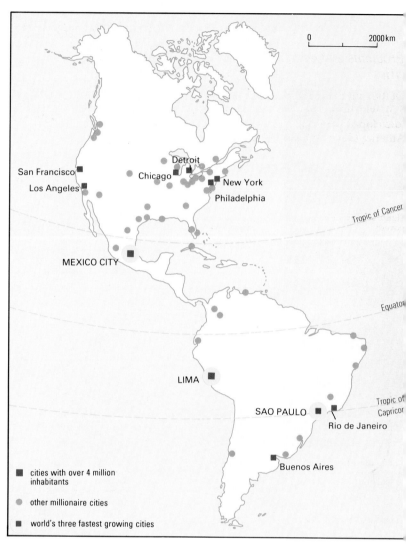

- ■ cities with over 4 million inhabitants
- ● other millionaire cities
- ■ world's three fastest growing cities

△ **Figure 5.1** Cities with over one million inhabitants, 1982

◁ **Figure 5.2** The world's large cities

Figures in millions

Latin America

Europe

North America

Asia

rank order	1970	1978	estimate 1985	estimate 2000
1	New York 16.5	New York 16.4	Tokyo 23.0	Mexico City 31.0
2	Tokyo 13.4	Tokyo 14.7	New York 18.0	Sao Paulo 26.0
3	London 10.5	Mexico City 14.0	Mexico City 17.9	Tokyo 24.0
4	Shanghai 10.0	Shanghai 10.9	Sao Paulo 16.8	Shanghai 23.0
5	Mexico City 8.6	Los Angeles 10.6	Shanghai 14.3	New York 22.0
6	Los Angeles 8.4	Paris 9.9	Los Angeles 13.7	Peking 19.0
7	Buenos Aires 8.4	Buenos Aires 8.4	Calcutta 12.1	Rio de Janeiro 18.0
8	Paris 8.4	Moscow 8.0	Bombay 12.1	Bombay 17.0
9	Sao Paulo 7.1	Chicago 7.7	Peking 12.0	Calcutta 16.0
10	Moscow 7.1	Peking 7.6	Buenos Aires 11.7	Jakarta 15.0
11	Peking 7.0	Sao Paulo 7.6	Rio de Janeiro 11.4	Seoul 15.0
12	Chicago 6.9	London 7.2	Seoul 11.2	Los Angeles 15.0

Problems and advantages of living in cities

Of the four photographs shown below (Figure 5.3), which two were taken in North America (developed world cities) and which two in Latin America (developing world cities)?

Figure 5.3 Wealth and poverty

▽ **A**

B ▷

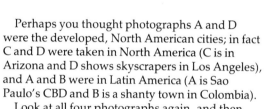

Perhaps you thought photographs A and D were the developed, North American cities; in fact C and D were taken in North America (C is in Arizona and D shows skyscrapers in Los Angeles), and A and B were in Latin America (A is Sao Paulo's CBD and B is a shanty town in Colombia).

Look at all four photographs again, and then list:

1 The problems associated with living in those four cities.

2 The advantages of living in those four cities.

▽ **C**

◁ **D**

Large urban areas in North America

Urban models

It has been suggested that towns do not grow in a haphazard way, but that they show certain generalised characteristics. For example, Burgess (Figure 5.4) suggested that most towns grew outward in a concentric pattern (he based his theory on such developed world cities as Chicago), wheras Hoyt (Figure 5.4) thought a 'wedge' shape was more typical of their growth. A model is a theoretical framework which may not actually exist, but which helps to explain the reality. Figure 5.5 illustrates a cross-section through a typical North American city.

Megalopolis

This means 'a very large city' and has for several decades been associated with New York. Nowadays the term is being linked to three large urban areas (Figure 5.6):

1 **'Boswash'** This extends from *Bos*ton to *Wash*ington DC (and so includes New York). Although covering only two per cent of the USA, it includes one fifth of the total population.

2 **'Chipitts'** This takes its name from *Chi*cago at the western end and *Pitts*burgh in the east. This has been the major industrial area of the USA for two centuries.

3 **'Sansan'** This is a newly emerging conurbation extending 1000 kilometres from *San* Francisco in the north through Los Angeles to *San* Diego in the south. In the centre is the still largely rural area of San Luis Obispo County with, as yet, no large city. *'To most Californians this is a long stretch of Highway 101 between Los Angeles and San Francisco. Now it is being "discovered" by urban dwellers due to its absence of conspicuous pollution, low crime rate, slower pace of life, mild, sunny, ocean-moderated climate, picturesque shoreline, mountains and valleys, and predominantly rural land uses. Retired people, tourists and the attendant service-providers are the major components of growth. It is this tertiary sector that is absorbing nearly all the working-age newcomers; manufacturing remains of only minor significance. Employment is stimulated by population growth, rather than growth having been stimulated by employment opportunities. Yet since 1970, the population growth rate of San Luis Obispo has been over four per cent, three times greater than the already high growth rate for the rest of California.'* (*Geographical Magazine*)

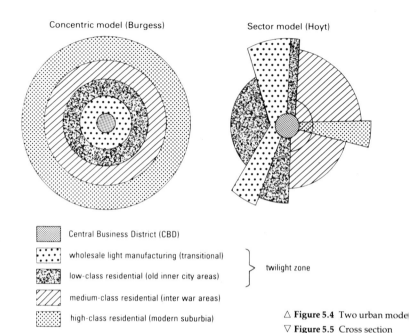

Concentric model (Burgess)   Sector model (Hoyt)

░░ Central Business District (CBD)

∷∷ wholesale light manufacturing (transitional) ⎫
                                                  ⎬ twilight zone
▒▒ low-class residential (old inner city areas) ⎭

╱╱ medium-class residential (inter war areas)

∴∴ high-class residential (modern suburbia)

△ **Figure 5.4** Two urban models

▽ **Figure 5.5** Cross section through a typical North American city

6   5   4   3   2   1   2   3   4   5   6
                       CBD
                   (skyscrapers)

2 tenement blocks of inner city ghettos

3 apartment blocks (mainly flats)

4 terraced houses

5 detached houses of suburbia

6 detached houses in commuter villages

▽ **Figure 5.6** North America's growing conurbations

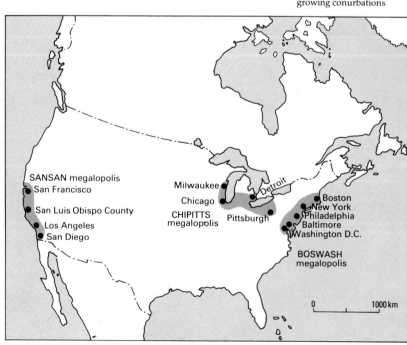

SANSAN megalopolis
San Francisco

San Luis Obispo County

Los Angeles
San Diego

Milwaukee
Chicago
CHIPITTS   Detroit
megalopolis   Pittsburgh

Boston
New York
Philadelphia
Baltimore
Washington D.C.

BOSWASH
megalopolis

0   1000 km

New York: a large city in the developed world

Figure 5.7 shows the site of New York City, and especially the central island of Manhattan (M on the photo) and Figure 5.8 gives the layout and the major buildings in Manhattan itself. In the foreground of the photo is the western end of Long Island (marked L) which is the major suburban and recreation area for New Yorkers. The skyscraper development has taken place in two distinct zones:

☐ MS is the area of midtown skyscrapers, which include the main hotels (the Plaza and Waldorf Astoria), shops (Fifth Avenue and Park Avenue), and theatres (Broadway).

☐ DS is the area of downtown skyscrapers, which include the financial and banking district (Wall Street and the Stock Exchange), the headquarters of advertising and publishing firms.

Three important buildings are the United Nations Building (UN), the Empire State Building (ESB) and the highest skyscraper in New York, the twin towers of the World Trade Centre (WT) which has 110 stories and reaches a height of 411 metres. On the plan of Manhattan notice the grid-iron layout of the roads, and the various methods of crossing the rivers on either side.

HM is Harlem, BR is the Bronx and CH is Chinatown.

▽ **Figure 5.7** New York

1 In which direction was the camera pointing in Figure 5.7?

2 Name the two rivers marked H and E; the state and city at NJ; the bridges B, MB and Q, and the large public park at C.

3 What were the advantages of the site of New York?

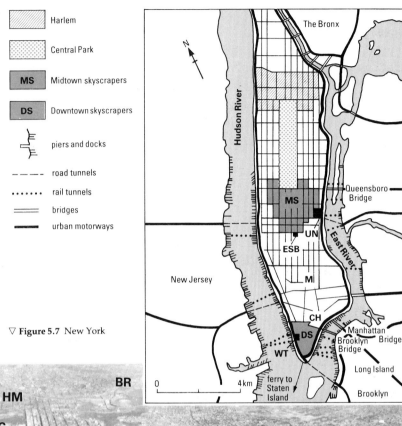

▽ **Figure 5.8** Plan of Manhattan (based on a diagram from *Geographical Studies in North America* by B. E. Price and E. Tweed; Oliver and Boyd)

43

Problems in the developed world

New York

New York is perhaps an extreme case, partly because of its size, but it does show most of the problems of large urban areas in the developed world.

- □ **High cost of land in the CBD** has led to skyscraper development (Figure 5.9) to try to make full use of area, and to try to satisfy the demand for a prime site. However, only highly successful firms can operate from here, e.g. the American Express credit card company, and leading oil companies.

- □ **Large companies moving out** The big companies who built the skyscrapers are themselves finding the cost and other environmental problems too great and are moving to out-of-town locations. Of 200 major companies located in the CBD in 1960, only 100 remained by 1980.

- □ **Traffic congestion** Each morning some two million commuters (people living outside Manhattan but working there) travel into the CBD, while at night the direction of movement is reversed.
  - (a) Although 75 per cent of these commuters travel by public transport (unlike those in other North American cities), high labour costs and financial losses are an annual problem.
  - (b) Cars still cause considerable noise and air pollution, as well as blocking the narrow canyon-like 'avenues' found between skyscrapers (Figure 5.10).
  - (c) Although Manhattan provided an ideal original defensive site, being surrounded by rivers, this now adds to the traffic congestion because all these commuters have to use the relatively few bridges and ferries or the underground (Figure 5.7 and 5.8).
  - (d) Numerous 'expressways' have had to be built, adding to the environmental problems.

- □ **Noise from aircraft** using the nearby Kennedy airport (Long Island) and La Guardia airport (to the east of the Bronx).

- □ **Increasing costs of services** As the more wealthy move away from the more central areas, those remaining have less money to pay for public services and yet are often those who need the extra services (e.g. hospitals).

- □ **Immigrants,** especially Negroes and Puerto Ricans, are caught up in the so-called 'vicious circle' of the ghetto (Figure 5.11). This leads to gang warfare and racial tension.

- □ **Urban decay** Many areas of working class houses were built, as in Britain, between 1860

△ **Figure 5.9** The Manhattan skyline, New York

▽ **Figure 5.10** The canyons of New York

and 1900. These tenement blocks, flats and terraced housing (Figure 5.5) have suffered from years of neglect (Figure 5.12). They have few modern amenities such as hot water, baths and garages, and suffer from damp. Many are rented, but when rents rise some may become unoccupied and are soon vandalised (Figure 5.12).

- □ **Crime** has increased dramatically in the ghetto areas with muggings and burglaries. On average New York has a murder every five hours.

- □ **Unemployment** has also increased rapidly with about one in seven (about 1½ million) out of work. This has increased as older industries (port and clothing) and services have declined.

Immigrants e.g. Puerto Ricans and Afro-Americans

Areas of poor quality housing

Lower educational standards in under-staffed slum schools

Mainly unskilled jobs. High rates of unemployment, crime and drug abuse

Lower than average income and high dependence on social security by the unemployed

◁ **Figure 5.11** The 'vicious circle' of the ghetto

▷ **Figure 5.12** Tenement blocks in Harlem

□ **Pollution** New York has a severe refuse collection and disposal problem, and the ghettos are full of litter and abandoned cars. Cars add to both air and noise pollution, while visual pollution includes run-down houses and graffiti (Figure 5.13).

□ **Water supply** Water has to be brought from some 200 kilometres away.

□ **Climate** Being a large city, New York becomes a 'heat island' in summer. Many well-off residents have second homes away from the city, but for those remaining the heat can be unbearable. New York also experiences blizzards in winter (adding to traffic congestion), while strong winds funnel down the 'canyons' between the skyscrapers.

□ **Threat of bankruptcy** as costs to run the city increase annually.

▷ **Figure 5.13** Graffiti on the New York underground

Latin American cities

On page 38 a number of reasons were given why people in Latin America, as well as in the rest of the developing world, were moving to urban areas. What happens when they arrive there?

Growth of 'spontaneous settlements' and 'shanty towns'

The migrants live in temporary, makeshift accommodation built tightly around the existing urban area. The people are 'squatters' in that they have no legal right to the land they occupy. The rapid growth of spontaneous settlements throughout the cities of the developing world has led to a range of local names. In Latin America they go under several names, e.g.

- □ **Favelas** in Brazil (Rio de Janeiro, Sao Paulo, Belo Horizonte)
- □ **Barriadas** in Peru (Lima)
- □ **Ranchos** in Venezuela (Caracas)
- □ **Callampas** in Chile (Santiago)
- □ **Colonias Proletarias** in Mexico (Mexico City)

In all of these settlements, squatters now account for over 40 per cent of the total population.

Sites for spontaneous settlements

- □ **Hillsides** As most of the flattest land is already used, makeshift accommodation spreads up hillsides in Lima (Figure 5.14), Rio de Janeiro and Caracas.

- □ **Rubbish tips** In Salvador (Brazil) rubbish thrown into the bay has accumulated to form sites for homes.

- □ **Mangrove swamps** Figure 5.15 shows bamboo catwalks in Guayaquil linking houses which have been built on stilts (also in Bahia in Brazil). Here few houses have lavatories, and then it is only a hole in the floor. The tide flushes the area twice a day, but as more rubbish and stones are thrown near the cat walks to try to create permanent roads the area is flushed less well, and this causes outbreaks of typhoid and dysentery (Figure 5.16).

The 'favelas' in Brazil

- □ **Accommodation** is often a collection of primitive shacks made from cardboard and corrugated iron, or possibly old blankets and sacking. Inside will be only a single room where the family lives, eats and sleeps. Most houses lack such basic amenities as electricity, gas, running water, toilets and main sewerage. The twin problems of the disposal of human waste, which is often left to run down the streets, and unhygienic washing conditions lead to disease. Between the houses the empty spaces become filled with rubbish because there is no refuse collection, though such empty spaces are soon filled by later migrants.

△ **Figure 5.14** Shanty town built on the hillsides around Lima, Peru

▽ **Figure 5.15** Guayaquil, Ecuador – the slums stretch out over the mangrove swamps, linked by catwalks

□ **Transport** Within the *favelas* the roads are only dirt tracks and open drains. Hardly anyone has a car. As shops and work are usually a long way off, public transport is essential but buses are few, if any.

□ **Food and clothes** Both are in short supply. The inhabitants are too poor to travel to, or shop in, the city centre. The goods in the few local food shops are exposed to dust and flies. Many families suffer from malnutrition, and virtually all from an unbalanced diet.

□ **Health** Disease, especially typhoid and dysentery, is spread easily because of the lack of clean water and proper sanitation, and the high density of houses and population. Medical provision (hospitals, doctors, nurses, drugs) is scanty and often too expensive for the patients. Infant mortality rates are high and life expectancy low.

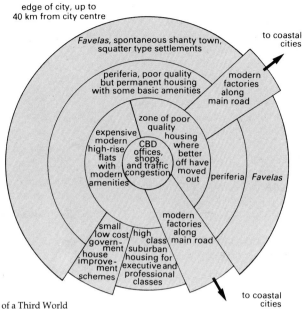

 **Figure 5.16** A spontaneous settlement in Guayaquil (both)   ▷ **Figure 5.17** Model for the development of a Third World city (based on Sao Paulo and Belo Horizonte)

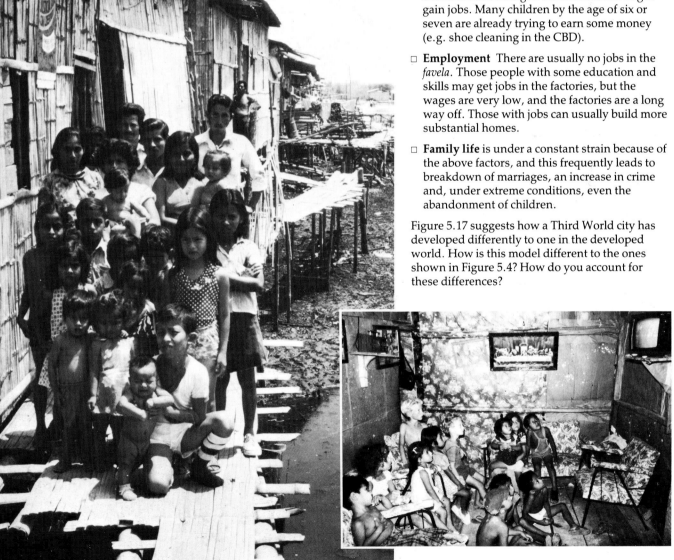

□ **Education** is also very limited. Children are left illiterate and lacking in the skills which might gain jobs. Many children by the age of six or seven are already trying to earn some money (e.g. shoe cleaning in the CBD).

□ **Employment** There are usually no jobs in the *favela*. Those people with some education and skills may get jobs in the factories, but the wages are very low, and the factories are a long way off. Those with jobs can usually build more substantial homes.

□ **Family life** is under a constant strain because of the above factors, and this frequently leads to breakdown of marriages, an increase in crime and, under extreme conditions, even the abandonment of children.

Figure 5.17 suggests how a Third World city has developed differently to one in the developed world. How is this model different to the ones shown in Figure 5.4? How do you account for these differences?

Improvement in Latin America

It must be stressed that not all parts of Latin American cities are *favelas*. Some parts have become as affluent as cities in North America, while others have, despite the lack of resources, made limited home improvements.

The CBD

It is difficult to tell the difference between Latin and North American city centres, for both have large office blocks (Figure 5.18), shops, entertainment and traffic jams (Figure 5.19).

Housing for the well-off

Although they are very much in a minority, each Latin American city has its well-off inhabitants (political leaders, army officers, businessmen, sport and pop stars). This group will live in expensive housing, ranging from elegant apartment complexes, each with its own social and recreational facilities, to Californian-style detached houses with large gardens and individual swimming pools. The family is probably limited to two children, housemaids will be employed, and security guards limit entry.

Organised and self-help housing projects

High-rise flats: the superblocks of Caracas (Figure 5.20). The authorities cleared many of the local *ranchos* (shanty towns) and built tower blocks which usually exceeded 15 storeys in height, containing between 150 and 450 two- or four-bedroomed apartments and with modern amenities such as electricity, water and main sewerage. But problems were created:

- Through using only a little space the areas became overcrowded.
- Through using land near to the CBD (convenient for jobs and shops) the superblocks were expensive to build, and so . . .
- Rents were often too high for the poorly paid or unemployed tenants to afford.
- Incoming residents, used to living in rural areas and then *ranchos*, had difficulty in adapting to high-rise living.

Self-help schemes These are schemes where the government, realising that 'shanty towns' cannot be removed, tries to help in low-cost improvements to the local environment. One scheme in Sao Paulo provides electricity, a water tank connected to the central water supply and in turn to an outside wash basin and an indoor bathroom/toilet. The buildings are of breeze block and are single storeyed (Figure 5.21).

The advantages of such self-help schemes are that they can be done in stages, they can create a community spirit, and the buildings can be erected relatively cheaply. However, such schemes also depend upon the desire and ability of the residents to plan, to co-operate and to carry out the improvements.

◁ **Figure 5.18** Sao Paulo's CBD
△ **Figure 5.19** Traffic congestion in Sao Paulo

▽ **Figure 5.20** Caracas - the high-rise blocks of the modern city. Some of the *ranchos* which still remain can be seen on the hillsides in the distance.

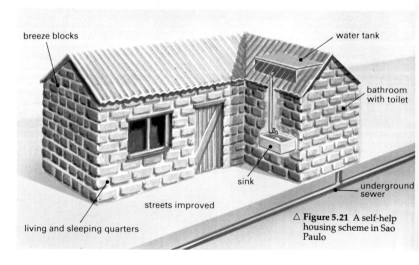

breeze blocks
water tank
bathroom with toilet
sink
underground sewer
streets improved
living and sleeping quarters

△ **Figure 5.21** A self-help housing scheme in Sao Paulo

Building new cities and reducing the importance of the primate city

Recent studies in Latin America have shown that many migrants leave their villages for small towns, and later take a second step to the largest city. A major problem of most Latin American countries is that they are dominated by one large or primate city, which usually is also the capital (e.g. Mexico, Guatemala, Chile). Here most of the economic growth takes place. In other countries (e.g. Brazil) with more than one large city, growth tends to take place either in particular parts of that country (Figure 5.22) e.g. Sao Paulo – Rio de Janeiro – Belo Horizonte, or on the coast (see Figure 5.22 for the distribution of cities with over one million inhabitants). Behind this are large areas where only small towns exist.

Would new cities help?

By creating planned cities the hope is to:

☐ absorb rural migrants and divert them from the primate city,

☐ offer greater job opportunities, and

☐ limit the social and environmental problems of the largest city.

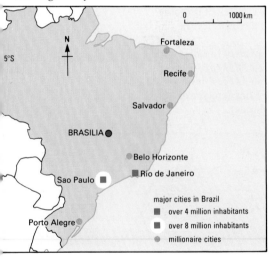

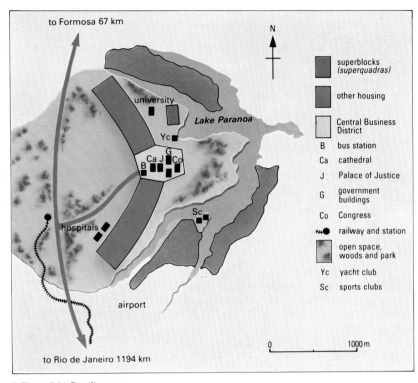

△ **Figure 5.24** Brasilia – open space in a new city. The city has been designed in the shape of an aeroplane.

◁ **Figure 5.22** Location of Brazilian cities

▽ **Figure 5.23** The planned open layout of Brasilia

▽ **Figure 5.25** The *favelas* of Brasilia (below right)

Brasilia

Brasilia was chosen, in 1952, to help open up the central areas of Brazil, and was inaugurated as the capital of Brazil (in place of Rio) in 1960. Since then its population has grown to over ¾ million (1980). It has been made the seat of government and has become a major tourist centre as a result of its futuristic architecture (Figure 5.23). In central residential areas both low-cost and luxury housing were built in the form of *super-quadras* (super blocks), which are self-contained and include shops, schools and clubs. Brasilia and its eight satellite towns now cover 8800 km². But

☐ It was designed for the motorist, not the pedestrian (distances to walk are considerable – Figure 5.24).

☐ The centres of industry, commerce, trade and culture have remained in Rio and Sao Paulo.

☐ Old problems soon reappear – lack of jobs and the emergence of *favelas* (Figure 5.25).

49

FOOD SUPPLY AND FARMING
Diet

A satisfactory diet has two important characteristics. It must:

(a) contain different types of food to build and maintain the body, and

(b) provide energy for the body to take part in work and leisure.

A balanced diet should contain:

- **Proteins,** such as meat, eggs and milk, to build and renew body tissues.

- **Carbohydrates**, such as cereals, sugar, fats, meat, eggs and potatoes, to provide energy.

- **Vitamins** and **minerals**, which prevent many diseases, and are found in dairy produce, fruit, meat, fish, eggs and vegetables.

In other words, the quality of the diet is as important as the quantity of food consumed. The amount of food required or consumed by a person is measured in calories.

Study Figures 6.1 and 6.2.

1 Which three countries have the most protein and calorie intake? What do you notice about the latitude of these three countries?

2 Which three countries have the least protein and calorie intake? What do you notice about the latitude of these countries?

Generally people in cooler, temperate regions need more calories per day (a minimum of 2600 calories per day in North America) than people living in hot, tropical climates (a minimum of 2300 calories per day in tropical Latin America). If these figures are true, 70 per cent of the world's population does not get enough to eat. In developing countries, there is a lack of protein, vitamins and minerals, and the basis for the diet is starchy carbohydrates.

It is especially the lack of protein in a diet which causes malnutrition (Figure 6.3). Figure 6.1 suggests that each person needs a minimum of 20 grammes of animal protein a day (some experts suggest it should be 30 grammes).

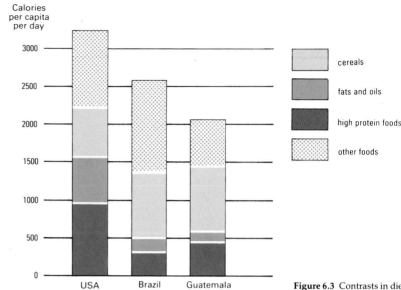

Figure 6.3 Contrasts in diet

Consumption of animal protein per person per day in grammes

USA	102.5
Uruguay	61.9
Chile	29.2
Mexico	23.4
Guatemala	8.5

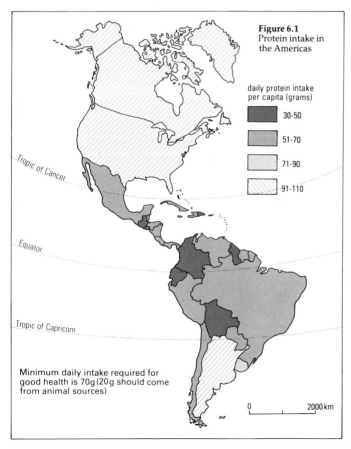

Figure 6.1 Protein intake in the Americas

daily protein intake per capita (grams)

- 30-50
- 51-70
- 71-90
- 91-110

Minimum daily intake required for good health is 70g (20g should come from animal sources)

0   2000 km

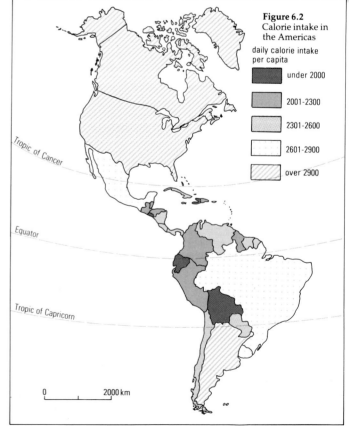

Figure 6.2 Calorie intake in the Americas

daily calorie intake per capita

- under 2000
- 2001-2300
- 2301-2600
- 2601-2900
- over 2900

0   2000 km

Of the world population

☐ (hatched) 1.5 billion people are well-fed and over-fed

☐ (grey) 1.6 billion sufficiently fed

☐ (dark) 1.4 billion under-nourished

S = threatened by starvation

0   2000 km

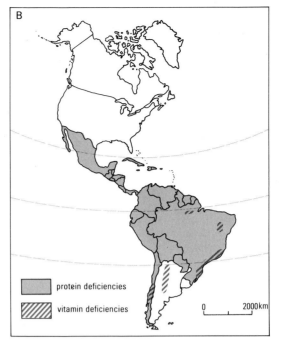

☐ protein deficiencies

☐ vitamin deficiencies

0   2000 km

◁ **Figure 6.4** The well-fed and the hungry

▽ **Figure 6.5** Major types of agriculture

The well-fed and the hungry (Figure 6.4)

Map A, using data from the United Nations, shows that only one-third of the population of the Americas is well fed. Most North Americans are extremely well fed, but in Latin America the unequal distribution of income and the general rise in world prices are making the problem worse.

Peru 1978

'Most of Peru's 16 million people are moving from malnutrition to the brink of starvation. An undernourished generation is growing up without the basic foods. You see them in the streets, pale and skinny. Peruvians have their main meal at mid-day. One father claims, "We used to have three dishes at lunch – a main course of chickpeas and lentils, and sometimes a little meat, fruit and a side dish of salad. Now we only have two dishes – soup, some beans, and perhaps fish, wheat and potatoes. We cannot afford apples and oranges."' (*The Guardian* 1978)

Map B in Figure 6.4 shows those parts of the Americas where the diet of the people is deficient in protein and vitamins.

Food and the farmer

Food supply depends upon the output of farmers. However, as Figure 6.5 shows, many parts of the Americas produce virtually no food at all, such as the tundra, coniferous forest, mountains, deserts and remoter areas of the equatorial forest. Other areas produce only the minimal amount for survival, mainly because of the adverse climates, soils and relief and insufficient money for good quality seed, animals and machinery. Only relatively few areas produce enough food both for themselves and to send to other, less fortunate areas. Figure 6.5 shows the location of the main types of farming in the Americas, and the remainder of this chapter describes the various farming systems and some problems and changes taking place within them.

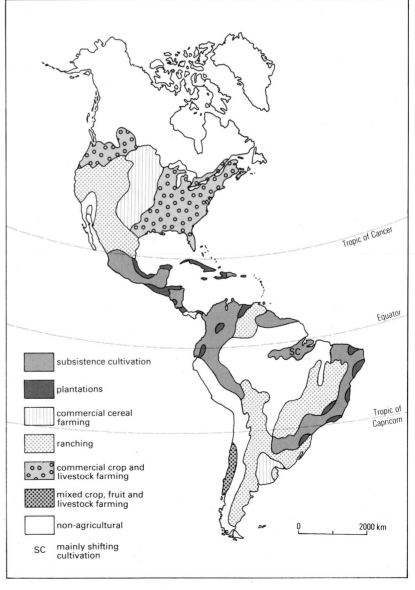

☐ subsistence cultivation

☐ plantations

☐ commercial cereal farming

☐ ranching

☐ commercial crop and livestock farming

☐ mixed crop, fruit and livestock farming

☐ non-agricultural

SC mainly shifting cultivation

0   2000 km

Tropical farming – subsistence

Subsistence farming is growing just enough for one's own family, but having nothing spare to sell. This, before European colonisation, was the traditional form of agriculture in the tropics. Areas where subsistence farming is still carried out today are shown in Figure 6.6. You will notice that they are in the less developed parts of the continent. A major type of farming within these subsistence areas is *shifting cultivation*.

Shifting cultivation in the Amazon Basin

This area is densely forested because of the extreme heat and high rainfall (page 16), and nature has developed a delicate plant–soil balance. Until very recently much of the land had been untitled (i.e. not belonging to anyone). In shifting cultivation:

- Trees are cut by stone axes and the area is burnt, leaving tree stumps exposed. The ash temporarily enriches the soil. This is known as 'slash and burn' (Figure 6.7) and is done by the men.

- In the clearings temporary houses are constructed of tree trunks with leaves for thatch, and built upon stilts to be above the frequently flooded ground.

- The women do most of the farming itself. Holes are dug and seeds or tubers are planted. In the hot, wet climate with an all-the-year growing season such crops as manioc, yams, beans and pumpkins can be grown. Manioc, the 'bread of the tropics', is used to produce a flour called cassava (Figure 6.8), as well as some sugar and poison for the men's darts. Manioc grows in poor soils, and is high in calories (carbohydrates) but low in protein – it takes six kilos of cassava to give as much protein as only 100 grammes of fish. Yams need richer soil but give twice as much protein as cassava.

- The food is for local consumption, and the only tool may be a hoe or an iron blade.

- The plant–soil balance is soon destroyed by heavy leaching (Figure 2.6), lack of humus renewal, soil erosion caused by the removal of the vegetation cover, and the lack of fertiliser and animal manure.

- Soil fertility and crop yields decline rapidly.

- The clearing has to be abandoned after 4 or 5 years and the Indians 'shift' to another part of the forest.

- A rapid, scrub-like, vegetation soon covers the clearing, but the impoverished soil cannot support trees.

Shifting cultivation needs a high labour input and large areas of land to provide food for just a few people. It is a wasteful method because it destroys both forest and soil, but in that environment permanent agriculture is out of balance with the climate.

Tropic of Cancer

Lowland Amerindians (e.g. Lacandons)

Lowland Amerindians (e.g. Boro, Megkronotis)

Equator

Highland Amerindians (Inca descendants)

Tropic of Capricorn

subsistence farming

0   2000 km

△ **Figure 6.6** Tropical subsistence agriculture (top)

△ **Figure 6.7** The 'slash and burn' technique of forest clearance in Colombia

In Central America – times of change

'The traditional style of Lacandon life was for each man to take his family and settle by a river or lake where his dwellings would be made as inconspicuous as possible. Settlement pattern was of dispersed clusters of two or three households. Since World War 2 modern Lacandons have been forced by outsiders to forsake their waterside locations. In 1976 there were only 360 Lacandon Indians living in three villages.'

In the Andes of Peru and Ecuador

Indian farmers still thresh corn by similar methods to the Incas. They exist on a subsistence, staple diet of potatoes, maize and barley, and by rearing llamas and alpacas. Little change has taken place in the last few centuries, and, although outlawed, an 'almost feudal . . . system of land tenure is still practised, involving labour and produce payments in return for the use of small plots of land. Where the Indian peasant has been given land it is often of poor quality, and without the backing of capital or technical advice he is usually unable to support his family. Coupled with a birth rate of 4.2 per cent, this has resulted in a move towards the urban centres of the mountain areas, where Indians are little better off, and earn low wages or simply beg in the streets.'

Is this the end of shifting cultivation and the traditional Indian way of life in the Amazon?

A recent newspaper report said:

'It is now possible to fly for three hours over what had been virgin forest only four years ago to see nothing but a desert of ash. In this charred wilderness lie the bones of millions of animals that once provided the Indian's food. Here some 300 ranches raising over six million Zebu cattle have been set up for quick profit (Figure 6.10). But the soil becomes rapidly impoverished and after three or four years the ranch is abandoned and all that is left is the barbed wire fencing.'

According to another report:

'A huge American company have built a giant pulp mill, and replaced many square kilometres of rainforest with a faster growing species. This one project provides almost 40,000 jobs.'

The taking over of much of the land by the cattle ranchers and timber companies has meant that the 'shifting cultivators' have been forced to 'settle' in permanent reservations where they have been 'encouraged' by the government to grow such cash crops as coffee, cocoa, palm oil and soya beans. So the Indians (page 33) are fighting for land and for their existence. Although forced to live on reservations, they still exhaust the soil within five years. They have two choices: they can cling to their old lives and be killed by ruthless invaders or die from 'western' diseases brought by those invaders; or they can move to join the other homeless and jobless in the *favelas* of the large urban areas. Shifting cultivation appears to be a rapidly dying system of farming.

◁ **Figure 6.8** Amerindian girls preparing manioc

Figure 6.9 (Main picture) Clearing in rainforest with traditional housing

△ **Figure 6.10** Zebu cattle, Brazil

Tropical farming – plantations

Plantations were developed in tropical parts of the world in the 18th and 19th centuries mainly by Europeans and North American merchants. The natural forest was cleared and a single crop (usually a bush or tree) was planted in rows (Figure 6.11). This so-called 'cash-crop' was grown for export, and was not used or consumed locally. Plantations needed a high capital investment to clear, drain and irrigate the land, to build estate roads, schools and hospitals, and to bridge the several years before the first crop could be harvested. Much manual labour was also needed so, although the managers were white, coloured labourers, obtained locally or often brought in from other countries, were used because they were both cheap and able to work in the hot, humid climate. The almost continuous growing season meant that the crop could be harvested virtually throughout the year. Today most plantations are still owned by 'multinational' companies, that is, companies with their headquarters in the developed, temperate latitude countries. The locations of the plantations in the Americas are seen in Figure 6.5.

1 The following companies have commercial links with plantations. With which crop is each associated: Fyffes, Dunlop, Cadbury, and Tate and Lyle?

2 (a) From your own knowledge, complete Figure 6.12.

   (b) Which is the only crop listed in Figure 6.12 which does not grow within the tropics of the Americas?

△ **Figure 6.11** A modern banana plantation in Ecuador

◁ **Figure 6.12** Location of various plantation crops

crop	major producing area in the Americas	other major areas in the world
rubber		
bananas		
tea		
sugar		
coffee		
cocoa		
palm oil		
cotton		
tobacco		
coconuts		

▽ **Figure 6.13** Coffee plantation

Coffee plantations (fazendas) in Brazil

The tree prefers to grow on gentle rolling ground or valley sides at altitudes up to 1700 metres (Figure 6.13). It does not like valleys which may become waterlogged, or act as frost hollows as frost is coffee's worst enemy. It grows best in a deep soil called *terra roxa*, in the major producing states of Parana, Sao Paulo and Minas Gerais. The tree begins to yield after three years, reaches a maximum between 10–15 years and dies after 30. When harvested, the red 'cherries', as the ripe coffee is called, are stripped from the branches and cut into half to expose two 'beans' which are left in the sun on huge drying yards. They are raked frequently, and large tarpaulins are kept nearby for protection against any rain.

Changes in coffee production

European (mainly Italian) immigrants in the 1870s developed new coffee fazendas. This led to an increase in coffee production. By 1906 Brazil produced 1.2 million tons of coffee when world demand was only 0.7 million, and coffee accounted for 70 per cent of Brazil's exports – two major problems! Meanwhile soils on the early plantations became exhausted and so new

fazendas were developed westwards into drier but less frosty areas. More immigrants in the 1960s again led to overproduction, but output was soon drastically cut by:

□ the government offering incentives for other crops to be grown,

□ the spread of a disease in coffee trees, and

□ a killing frost in 1976.

While Brazil had produced 43 million bags of coffee and 49 per cent of the world's total in 1960, she only produced 20 million bags and 26 per cent of the world's total in 1980.

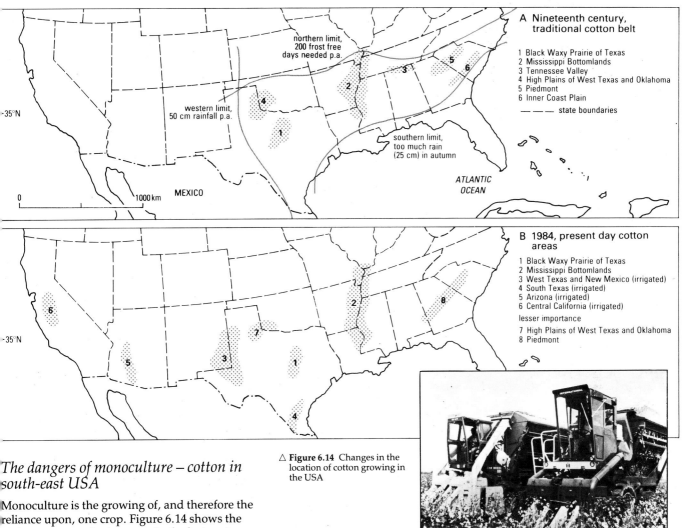

A Nineteenth century, traditional cotton belt

northern limit,
200 frost free
days needed p.a.

western limit,
50 cm rainfall p.a.

southern limit,
too much rain
(25 cm) in autumn

-35°N

0   1000 km   MEXICO

ATLANTIC
OCEAN

1 Black Waxy Prairie of Texas
2 Mississippi Bottomlands
3 Tennessee Valley
4 High Plains of West Texas and Oklahoma
5 Piedmont
6 Inner Coast Plain
– – – – state boundaries

B 1984, present day cotton areas

-35°N

1 Black Waxy Prairie of Texas
2 Mississippi Bottomlands
3 West Texas and New Mexico (irrigated)
4 South Texas (irrigated)
5 Arizona (irrigated)
6 Central California (irrigated)
lesser importance
7 High Plains of West Texas and Oklahoma
8 Piedmont

△ **Figure 6.14** Changes in the location of cotton growing in the USA

△ **Figure 6.15** Cotton harvesters

The dangers of monoculture – cotton in south-east USA

Monoculture is the growing of, and therefore the reliance upon, one crop. Figure 6.14 shows the major cotton producing areas in the last century. With the exception of the Mississippi Valley, these areas have declined and, as Figure 6.14 also shows, newer areas have developed.

Why did cotton, often grown as a single crop, decline in the 'Southern' states?

- There was a tendency to overproduce.

- Growing the same crop each year takes the same minerals from the soil and causes exhaustion.

- Cotton was often grown on steep slopes which had been deforested, and this encouraged soil erosion.

- The plant was attacked by a pest called the boll weevil which thrived in the hot, wet climate. The weevil laid its eggs in the cotton boll, and after hatching the larvae destroyed the fibres before flying away to lay more eggs.

- An extreme of climate could restrict output one year, and the farmer had no alternative source of income.

- World prices and demand tended to fluctuate.

- Labour became short as many negroes moved to urban areas hoping for better paid jobs.

- There was competition from synthetic fibres.

- Increased mechanisation (Figure 6.15) enabled the farmer to grow a wider range of crops.

Plantation agriculture today

- Tree crops are grown as an 'umbrella' to prevent soil erosion and leaching.

- In new areas, the crop is substituted only gradually for the natural forest.

- Between the rows, smaller bushes and plants are used to help cover the soil, and later these add humus to the soil.

- There is a return to hoeing and hand planting, because the European plough tended to go too deep and increased the risk of erosion.

- Increased mechanisation (Figure 6.15) has reduced the amount of labour needed.

- Insecticides and fertilisers are sprayed from aeroplanes.

- Some large estates have been subdivided to help some of the landless of the country.

- Attempts are made to process the crop rather than to export it in its raw state.

But has plantation agriculture –

(a) been a benefit to the country by employing more labour?

(b) helped or hindered the development of the country?

Temperate latitudes – cereals

Figure 6.16 shows the flat relief of the Prairies and the extensive use made of the land for wheat farming. The North American wheatfields (Figure 6.18) provide much of the wheat needed by, traditionally, Western Europe, and now increasingly by the USSR and the East Asian countries of China, Japan and Taiwan (Figure 6.17).

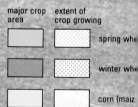

The Canadian Prairies

The Amerindians of these plains used the natural grassland vegetation for hunting bison. When the first colonists arrived, they drove the Indians away and brought cattle to graze on large ranches. Later, as the world price for cereals increased, the demand by the industrialised western European countries rose, and the trans-American railways were completed, vast areas of land were ploughed up and given over to wheat.

However, the climate was not overfavourable to wheat cultivation. Look again at the graph for Saskatoon in Figure 2.1, and read again page 24 to make sure you know why the American Mid-West and prairies have limited and unreliable rainfall (even periods of drought); hail and summer storms; long winters and blizzards; a short growing season; and strong winds causing soil erosion.

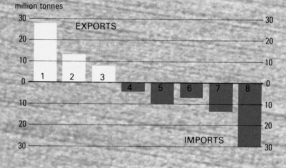

1	USA
2	Canada
3	Australia
4	Western Europe
5	Eastern Europe
6	Latin America
7	Africa
8	Asia

Figure 6.16 (Main picture) Wheat farming on the Prairies, Colorado

△ **Figure 6.17** World trade in wheat, 1977–78

◁ **Figure 6.18** Major wheat and corn growing areas in North America

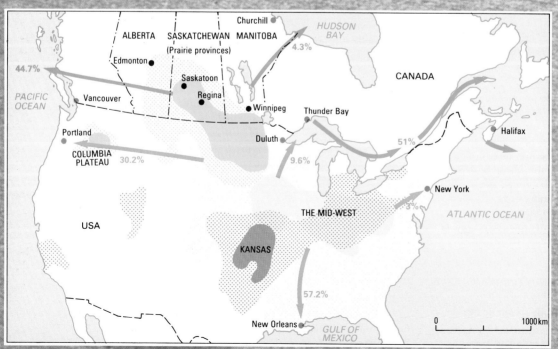

How the physical conditions favour the growth of wheat

☐ Summers, although short, are warm and sunny enabling the crop to ripen.

☐ The long hours of daylight in summer help the ripening.

☐ Winter frosts break up the soil.

☐ Rainfall is light and adequate, fortunately coming mainly in the growing season.

☐ The 'chinook', a warm, dry south-westerly wind, (Figure 2.33) helps to melt the snow in spring.

☐ The black soils (chernozems) of the prairies are deep, and get their colour from the rich humus which resulted from the decay of the original grassland cover.

☐ The almost level plains help mechanisation and transportation.

How wheat yields have increased

☐ Because of the flatness of relief, both roads and railways, together with field boundaries, were built in straight lines. The land was divided into sections each of which measured one square mile (1.6 square kilometres). In the wetter east each farm was given a quarter or a half section, and in the drier west at least one full section. In most cases these sections proved too small, many farmers left, and sections were amalgamated into more economic units.

☐ Drought and frost resistant seeds have been developed to reduce the climate risk.

☐ Quicker maturing seeds mean that wheat needs a growing season of only 90 days.

☐ Strip farming where land is ploughed at right angles to the wind, or where wheat and grass are grown in alternate strips.

☐ Increased mechanisation (Figure 6.19). At harvest time teams of workers move northwards from Texas into Saskatchewan. Both tractors and combines have headlights and arc lights to enable long hours to be worked.

☐ Dry farming methods where seeds are planted deeper, and 'trash' farming where stubble is left to protect the soil. A machine called a sub-surface cultivator, consisting of sharp blades, cuts off weeds at root level.

☐ Irrigation from the Saskatchewan river and its tributaries which reach a peak flow after the spring snow melt, a time coinciding with plant germination.

☐ Government grants.

☐ An increase in ranching, crop rotation, and alternative crops.

☐ Improved storage (in elevators) and transport reducing the amount of wheat lost.

☐ Improved fertilisers (including manure from the reintroduced cattle) and pesticides (controlling the previous grasshopper swarms).

☐ Trees planted as windbreaks.

The prairies are part of the spring wheat belt (Figure 6.18), the season in which the seeds are planted. Further south is the corn (or maize) belt which also contains most of America's pigs (or hogs), and the winter wheat belt where seeds can be sown in the autumn because the winters are less severe than in Canada.

△ **Figure 6.19** Mechanised harvesting on the Prairies (top)

Temperate latitudes – stock rearing

▽ **Figure 6.20** The Pampas

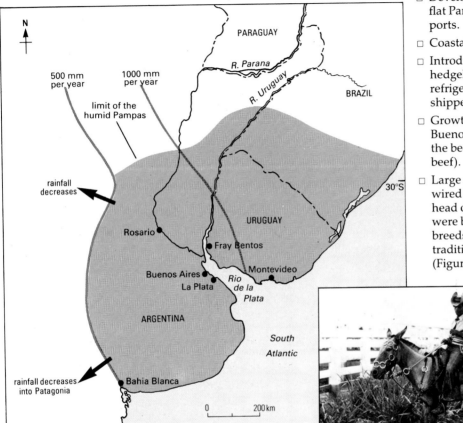

Development of beef farming (estancias)

□ Natural grasses were replaced by alfalfa (a leguminous, moisture retaining crop) and other fodder crops.

□ Development of a dense rail network over the flat Pampas linking it with the Rio de la Plata ports.

□ Coastal access for export to industrial countries.

□ Introduction of barbed wire (for fencing on the hedgeless Pampas) in the 1870s; tin cans and refrigeration (enabling frozen meat to be shipped to Europe).

□ Growth of 'frigorificos' in such ports as Rosario, Buenos Aires and Fray Bentos which process the beef into numerous products (e.g. corned beef).

□ Large estancias (ranches), divided into huge wired paddocks. Some estancias keep 20 000 head of carefully selected cattle. Pedigree bulls were brought from Europe to improve local breeds. The estancia stockmen are still the traditional South American cowboy or Gaucho (Figure 6.21).

◁ **Figure 6.21** South American Gaucho

▽ **Figure 6.22** The inhospitable Falkland Islands

Argentina and Uruguay

In temperate latitudes as rainfall decreases, making the growing of cereals and the production of milk more difficult, farmers turn more to the rearing of animals for meat. On the Pampas (Figure 6.20):

□ In the wetter extreme east (about 1000 mm of rain per year) maize, wheat and dairy cattle are most important.

□ Westwards and southwards as rainfall decreases, beef cattle predominate together with some fodder crops (alfalfa) and wheat.

□ Where rainfall is below 500 mm a year, grass becomes too poor for cattle, and sheep farming takes over, e.g. in Patagonia in southern Argentina.

Advantages of the Pampas for beef ranching

Climatically (see page 22, Figure 2.1) summers are very warm and humid, winters temperate and wet. Almost continuous plant growth is encouraged by the amounts and distribution of the rainfall and by the temperatures, which are high during most of the year. The land is flat and, especially in Argentina, soils are deep and rich – many being alluvial, having been brought down by such rivers as the Parana and Uruguay (Figure 6.20).

Sheep farming in Patagonia and the Falkland Islands

Sheep replace cattle as the climate deteriorates.

□ Patagonia (South Argentina) is a very dry area.

□ The Falkland Islands (where wool is the major export) are suited to sheep if only because the low annual temperatures, heavy rain, strong winds, poor grass and thin soils make all other forms of farming impossible (Figure 6.22).

As elsewhere in Latin America, most land is owned by absentee landlords. On the islands the biggest is the Falkland Island Company which owns 40 per cent of the land, rears 300,000 sheep, employs 250 people, and runs shops.

Market gardening – California

Intensive farming is making the maximum use of the land. Market gardening or, as the Americans call it, truck farming is the growing of fruit, flowers and vegetables. It requires high inputs, but it usually gives a good profit.

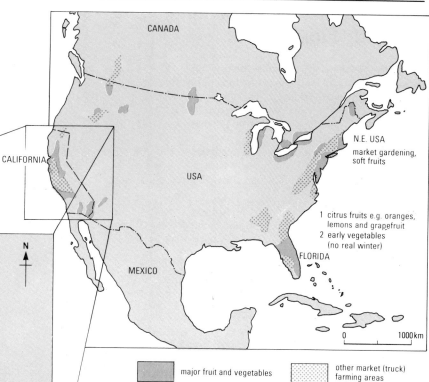

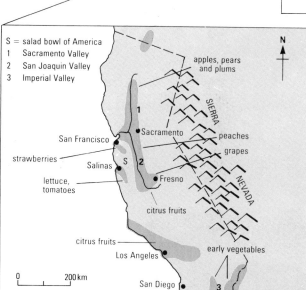

S = salad bowl of America
1 Sacramento Valley
2 San Joaquin Valley
3 Imperial Valley

△ **Figure 6.23** Market gardening in the USA

◁ **Figure 6.24** Seasonal Mexican labourers picking food crops in the Imperial Valley south of the Salton Sea

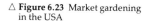

▽ **Figure 6.25** Harvesting grapes in the Napa Valley

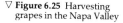

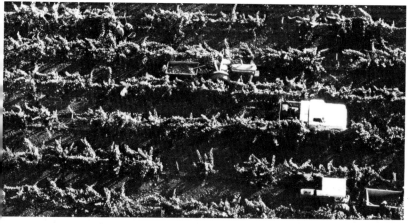

Physical factors favour market gardening in California:

☐ Hot, sunny, dry summers.

☐ Mild winters caused by the nearness of the sea, and the Sierra Nevada (Figure 6.23) holding cold continental air back.

☐ Alluvial soils and flat valley floors.

☐ Availability of irrigation (page 68) to overcome the summer drought.

Human-economic factors, however, are much more important:

☐ Nearness to urban markets, especially as these areas have a high standard of living.

☐ Access to main roads and a railway to deliver the produce fresh to the market.

☐ Availability of labour supply – especially seasonal labour. California receives much of this from Mexico (Figure 6.24).

☐ Highly mechanised machinery for harvesting and packaging (Figure 6.25). The Americans call this intensive mechanisation 'agribusiness'.

The main crops, and their location in California, are shown on Figure 6.23.

Hobby farming is increasing rapidly in North America. It is the buying of farms and farmland by city workers who intend to go on earning the bulk of their income from their city work. The farms they buy must lie within commuting distance of the city, and preferably in attractive areas because the beauty of the landscape is considered more important than its commercial use. The new owners tend to spend money on improving the farm buildings rather than the land, and may rent out parts of their holdings that they do not wish to farm themselves.

Land use

In 1826 the German agriculturalist Johann von Thünen suggested a land use model for a flat plain of equal fertility surrounding a city. He suggested that these factors: the yield per unit of area, the bulk of the product, the distance from the market and the cost of transport to it, market prices, and the amount of attention the product needed, would together mean that the types of land use around the city would be in distinct zones (Figure 6.26).

☐ Next to the city the farmer concentrates upon perishable, fragile and bulky products such as fruit, vegetables and milk (dairy cows need attention twice daily).

☐ With increasing distance from the city come: land for timber (a bulky product but an essential fuel in 1826!); cereals, because they need less attention than market garden produce; and finally the raising of animals.

Being a model it is not necessarily found in reality; it is even less likely 150 years after its suggestion, and in a world in which flat plains of equal fertility rarely exist. The nearest is perhaps Uruguay, and Figure 6.27 shows the land use of that country. Study both Figures 6.26 and 6.27.

1 How closely does Uruguay fit von Thünen's model?

2 Does a similar model exist around your own local town or city?

Methods of increasing food production

There are two basic problems:

(a) Only 10 per cent of the earth's surface can be cultivated (70 per cent is water, 10 per cent desert, and 10 per cent mountains and ice).

(b) The world's population is increasing rapidly.

So how can more people be fed on the same amount of land? Below is a list of suggested methods which you could discuss in class, or at least think about for yourself.

☐ Maintaining and improving soil fertility and reducing soil erosion (see Chapter 15).

☐ Careful control and use of water (Chapter 8).

☐ Improving plant and animal breeding, e.g. higher yielding seeds, drought and disease resistant seeds, better breeds of animals.

☐ Control of pests and disease (Chapter 7).

☐ Increased mechanisation and equipment – providing that they are suitable for the environment.

☐ Better storage, transport and processing methods. It is estimated that 25 per cent of harvested crops in developing countries are lost to animals, mould, etc.

☐ Sharing out land more evenly.

☐ Improving farm management and creating farmers' co-operatives.

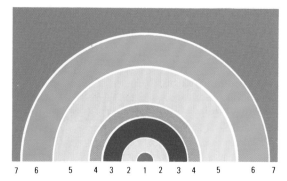

◁ **Figure 6.26** Von Thünen's land use model

1 city
2 market gardening
3 firewood and timber
4 intensive arable (cereals)
5 cereals with some pasture (cattle)
6 three field system
7 livestock farming (beef and sheep)

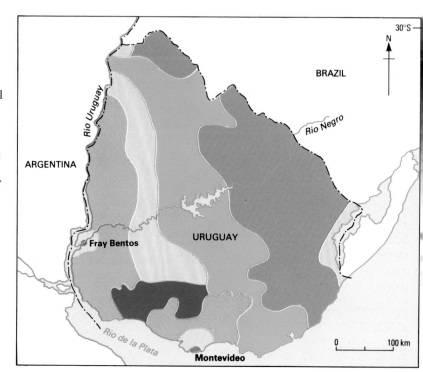

△ **Figure 6.27** Land use in Uruguay

☐ urban areas
☐ market gardening (orchard and vines)
☐ dairying
☐ intensive cereals (arable)
☐ cereals with livestock
☐ extensive sheep grazing
☐ extensive cattle ranching (beef)

☐ Increasing protein – lack of protein is a major cause of malnutrition.

☐ Increasing fish foods (page 61).

☐ Raising standards of living in rural areas so as to prevent rural depopulation.

☐ Reclaiming land from the sea, desert fringes, marsh, etc.

☐ Improving grassland so that animal products can increase in quality and quantity.

☐ Diversification of farming to reduce monoculture in an area, and the reliance of a country on one export crop (page 55).

☐ More aid from the developed world for the developing countries.

☐ Continued agricultural research and development.

FOOD SUPPLY AND FARMING
Fish as a source of food

Peru

Fish provide protein, a major source in overcoming malnutrition. Fish only exist in certain parts of the sea (the shallow continental shelves where sunlight can allow plankton to live). Figure 6.28 shows how upwellings of cold water from the Peru–Chile trench bring nutrients and plankton to the surface, and so provide food for such fish as the anchovy.

- Before 1950 the numerous fish off Peru were the diet of a huge bird colony, which in turn produced vast amounts of guano (droppings) which had accumulated to several metres thick and was sold as a fertiliser.

- In the 1950s anchovy were caught, processed at such ports as Chimbote and Callao and sent as fishmeal for cattle in North America and Europe. One million tons of fish a year were caught.

- By 1970 Peru caught ten million tons of fish, more than any other country in the world. Of this, 98 per cent was processed and exported (how typical was this for a developing country?) There were 150 processing plants, 1000 boats and 40 000 people in employment.

- By 1972 there was a fall in the catch due to overfishing.

- After 1976 came a total collapse due to the continual presence of the warm current known as 'El Niño' ('The Christmas Child'). It gets it name because it normally arrives each year just after Christmas. It brings from the north warm water which is lacking in oxygen, nutrients and plankton, and so causes fish to migrate and the birds that feed on them to die of starvation. It also brings heavy rain to the Atacama Desert.

- Normally, El Niño stays for only a few weeks, but since 1976 it has remained (as happens every ten years or so). This has meant:

- Less protein for the Peruvians.

- The closure of fishmeal factories.

- North America and Europe having to use grain for their cattle food, reducing some of their grain exports to the developing countries.

◁ **Figure 6.29** The fishing port of Ramea, Newfoundland

The future for Peru

- A hope that 'El Niño' will retreat and will be replaced by the cold Humboldt current.

- The Peruvians could catch other fish than anchovy.

- Conservation methods (e.g. limiting the season and the size of the catch) could be applied.

Newfoundland

Newfoundland also relies on fishing because of the lack of land resources. The cold climate, poor soils, lack of farmland (only 0.2 per cent of the island) and therefore food supply, and a lack of jobs (Figure 6.29), meant the islanders had either to turn to the sea, or move elsewhere. They chose the sea. Fortunately the island was adjacent to the Grand Banks (part of the continental shelf) where the sea is rich in plankton (because of the meeting of the warm Gulf Stream and cold Labrador currents) and provides rich fishing grounds for cod, hake and herring.

More fish and more protein for the world

Yields can be increased but great care is needed so as not to overfish. Fish are unlikely to become extinct; but as more are caught each year they are living shorter lives and therefore producing fewer young, and being caught younger they are smaller in size and weight.

▽ **Figure 6.28** Fishing off the Peruvian coast

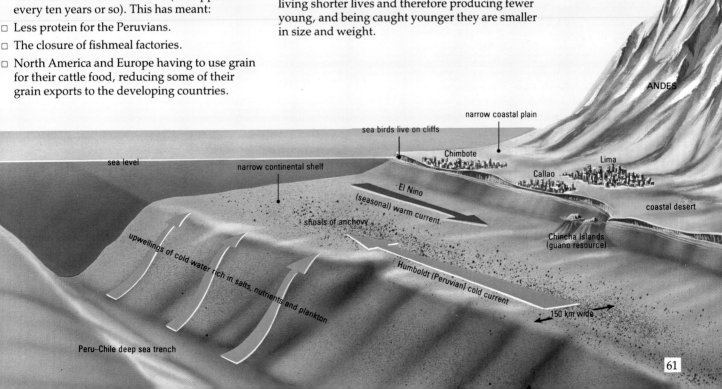

ANDES

narrow coastal plain

sea birds live on cliffs

Chimbote

Lima

Callao

coastal desert

sea level

narrow continental shelf

El Nino (seasonal) warm current

shoals of anchovy

Chincha Islands (guano resource)

upwellings of cold water rich in salts, nutrients and plankton

Humboldt (Peruvian) cold current

150 km wide

Peru–Chile deep sea trench

Major diseases

Already in this book reference has been made several times to poor health, poor diet and disease in the developing countries. Figure 7.1 shows some of the major diseases and causes of death in the Americas and, along with Figure 7.2, emphasises the differences between the causes of death in the more affluent, developed North America and in the poorer, less developed countries of Latin America.

Diet deficiency diseases

These are directly related to a lack of necessary proteins (Figure 6.1), vitamins and minerals which help to give sufficient calories (energy) per day (Figure 6.2). About two-thirds of the world's population eat insufficient food in terms of quality and quantity, and so become undernourished and suffer from malnutrition. Being ill-fed may not cause actual death, but it lowers the resistance of the body to other diseases which may be the ultimate cause of death. The United Nations Organisation lists the Andean countries as one of the three world areas suffering most from deficiency diseases.

Lack of protein
Those areas in Latin America suffering a lack of protein were shown in Figure 6.1. Lack of protein causes *kwashiorkor*, which is recognisable by a swollen and distended belly (Figure 7.3), thinning hair, pale colour, and a deterioration of the brain. It causes apathy and lack of energy which lowers resistance to other diseases and therefore death if untreated (Figure 7.4). *Marasmus* is a similar disease caused mainly through starvation, but does not have the same degree of belly swelling.

Water-borne diseases

Bilharzia, which affects some 200 million people in the world, is caused by parasitic worms which actually use the Bilharzia snail as their host. Figure 7.5 explains how the eggs of this worm may eventually reach humans. Within two or three weeks of the worms entering the body (usually through the feet as people walk, wash or swim in infected water), the victim develops headaches and fever. Two or three months later there may be blood in the urine, and eventually inflammation of the liver and serious bladder and kidney problems.

Malaria causes fever and weakness. It is caused by the female anopheles mosquito biting an infected person and carrying the parasites to another person's blood stream. Mosquitos live in warm, wet climates, and especially in stagnant water. (See Figure 7.6 for location.)

Yellow Fever produces fever, aching limbs and head, jaundice and vomiting. It too can kill if untreated.

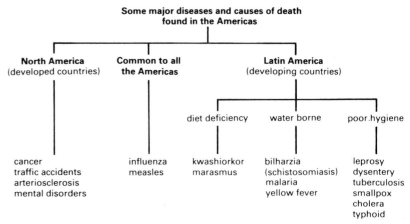

Some major diseases and causes of death found in the Americas

N.B. In Brazil the major causes of death in the large urban areas are the same as in North America (developed countries)

△ **Figure 7.1**

◁ **Figure 7.2** Causes of death in North and Latin America

Cause	Developed countries (%)	Developing countries (%)
diseases of early infancy	6	22
infectious diseases	4	21
heart disease	39	5
cancer	18	3
brain diseases	14	2
traffic accidents	7	3

◁ **Figure 7.3** How hunger kills

Calorie intake drops below daily expenditure of energy

If effort continues to be expended at the same rate the victims burn up their own body fats, muscles and tissues for fuel

Starvation begins when people lose 30% of their body weight

Resistance to disease is lowered. People often die as a result of disease rather than starving to death

Kidneys, liver (and endocrine system) cease to function properly

Shortage of carbohydrates affects the mind causing confusion, and also causes great lassitude

Other diseases

Other diseases include *dysentery* (often a result of a lack of sanitation), *trachoma* (an irritation of the eyes and eventual blindness), *leprosy*, *tuberculosis* and *smallpox*.

1 Using Figure 7.1 and 7.2, describe and give reasons for the differences between the major causes of death in North America and Latin America.

2 How is it possible to reduce the number of

   (a) nutritional diseases,

   (b) water-borne diseases,

   (c) dysentery cases?

3 What do you notice about the distribution of the five illnesses shown in Figure 7.6?

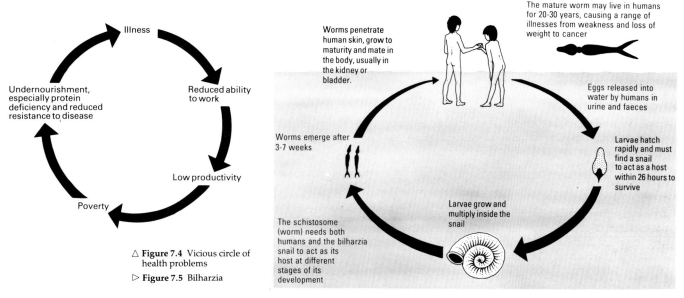

△ **Figure 7.4** Vicious circle of health problems

▷ **Figure 7.5** Bilharzia

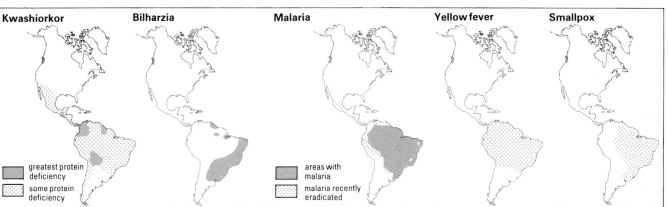

△ **Figure 7.6** Distribution of selected diseases in the Americas

Health services

It has been pointed out that most of the above diseases do not necessarily cause death themselves, but reduce resistance to other diseases, and can eventually cause death if untreated. Unfortunately these diseases are most common in the poorer countries of the world – those which have –

☐ the least money to spend on building hospitals and providing drugs,

☐ the least education, which may mean fewer doctors (Figure 7.7) and nurses, and also less knowledge among the people about how to avoid and treat basic diseases,

☐ the poorest transport facilities, making it difficult for patients to reach doctors and hospitals, and

☐ the lowest incomes, meaning that families cannot afford to pay for doctors or drugs.

The World Health Organisation is trying to break the vicious circle of poverty shown in Figure 7.4, yet as infant mortality rates fall and life expectancy increases this means there are even more patients needing treatment, thus adding to the overloaded health facilities. Existing health facilities in developing countries tend to be in urban rather than rural areas.

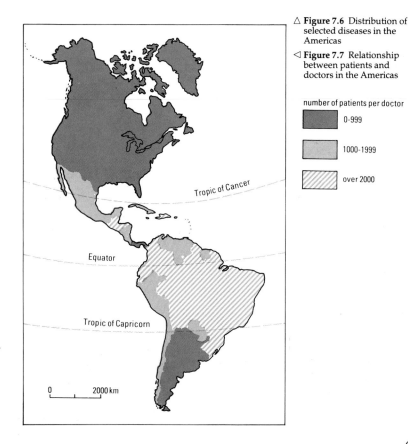

◁ **Figure 7.7** Relationship between patients and doctors in the Americas

number of patients per doctor

■	0-999
▨	1000-1999
▨	over 2000

63

Demand and supply

Figure 8.1 contrasts some differences between demand and supply in North and Latin America. Water is essential for life – without it the land is desert and uninhabited. Figure 8.2 is part of the Atacama Desert in Peru – only coming to life when a river from snow melt in the Andes crosses it. Peru is prepared to pay enormous sums to obtain water (Figure 8.3). It was thought that by building huge reservoirs to provide water the country would improve its standard of living (Figure 8.4) – but see page 66 for what really happened.

A predominantly British consortium of consulting engineers has won the design contract for a grandiose £250 million scheme to transfer water across the Andes to the Peruvian capital, Lima. The award could lead to orders for British contractors for hydro-electric and pumping stations which will be needed to carry the water from the River Mantaro, on the eastern side of the Andes, across Peru's "Great Divide" to Lima.

The scheme, which has been under discussion since the late '60s, will aim to meet Lima's water requirements until the end of the century and substantially increase electricity production in the highlands. It will involve pumping water up the eastern side of the cordillera to altitudes of up to 5000 metres, enlarging the capacity of Lake Junin, building new reservoirs and then transferring water through the trans-Andean tunnel and down to Lima on the Pacific.

△ **Figure 8.3** This news item from *The Guardian* describes Peru's £250 million plan for water

	North America	Latin America
Demand (litres per person per day)	400 for domestic use; 5000 in California (including industrial and farming use)	20 in the least developed countries
Uses	Domestic (drinking, washing, swimming); irrigation (crops and pasture); industry (power, cooling, washing, waste)	Domestic (drinking, washing); limited irrigation
How water is obtained	Collected in reservoirs, transferred by pipes to individual homes and factories	Water holes (in extreme rural areas); standpipes (one for perhaps 50 families in urban areas); individual taps only in wealthy parts of cities
Problems of supply and demand	Reliable rainfall not always in areas of highest demand Certain areas have seasonal droughts (cost of expensive reservoirs) Huge demand means water is being diverted many kilometres (p68)	In rural areas a long walk to the well or water hole Contaminated supplies affect health (Ch.7) No means of storage during seasonal and prolonged droughts Few homes have running water or sewers Lack of money for big schemes (Figure 8.12), which even when in operation only benefit a few people (p 66) Desertification now affects 19% of earth's surface, and 80 million people (Figure 2.12) — it is caused by over-cultivation, over-grazing and improper irrigation

◁ **Figure 8.1** Contrasts in supply and demand of water between North and Latin America

▽ **Figure 8.2** Irrigated valley in Cuzco, Peru

Clean water for all by 1990?

The United Nations Organisation (UNO) estimates that 80 per cent of all diseases in developing world countries are due to unsafe water supply and inadequate sanitation (Figures 8.5 and 8.6). Two major problems are:

1 (a) Rural areas are much less well off than urban areas, usually because planners, politicians and bureaucrats live in the towns. Rural people tend to be poor and illiterate, to lack political power and, to the decision maker, to live in small villages which do not seem to justify any large capital investment (page 38).

(b) The urban fringe, consisting often of new migrants in squatter settlements and shanty towns (page 46), may be even worse off than many villages. One standpipe may serve many families, and spillages may form stagnant pools which become breeding grounds for mosquitoes and other insects. The lack of sanitation often means that the roads are open sewers.

2 Although between 1962 and 1975 the percentage of urban inhabitants served with clean water improved by 20 per cent in South-East Asia, in Latin America and the Caribbean Islands it *declined* by 10 per cent.

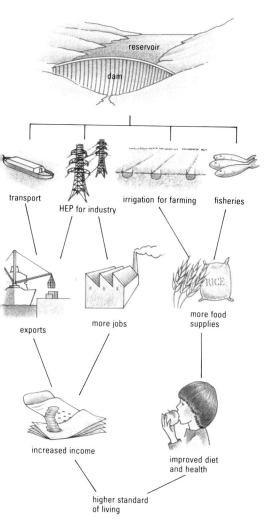

transport

HEP for industry

irrigation for farming

fisheries

exports

more jobs

more food supplies

increased income

improved diet and health

higher standard of living

△ **Figure 8.4** Creating reservoirs to aid development

◁ **Figure 8.6** The World Health Organization reports on water supply in the developing world

▽ **Figure 8.7** Charcoal water filter

△ **Figure 8.5** In La Salada, a poverty stricken village in Colombia, the people must drink stagnant rainwater or the foul waters of the River Bogota. They try to purify it by adding ashes or crushed cactus leaves

At the 1977 UN Water Conference it was urged that all countries should produce national plans by 1980, and that the period 1980–1990 should be called 'The International Drinking Water Supply and Sanitation Decade' (Figure 8.6).

Education is essential – people need to know how to store water to avoid contamination at home, and to know that they cannot drink water from any source just because they are thirsty, and that they must not pollute fresh supplies. In return they need cheap ways of obtaining fresh water using low technology, such as the charcoal water filter shown in Figure 8.7.

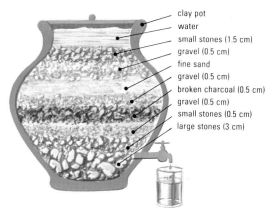

clay pot
water
small stones (1.5 cm)
gravel (0.5 cm)
fine sand
gravel (0.5 cm)
broken charcoal (0.5 cm)
gravel (0.5 cm)
small stones (0.5 cm)
large stones (3 cm)

All materials required for the water filter are obtained from local sources (excluding the tap). The twenty litre clay pot contains graded layers of stones, gravel, sand and broken charcoal and acts as an effective filter for solids and other pollutants. Only one pot is needed to filter sufficient drinking water for one family.

Water in Latin America

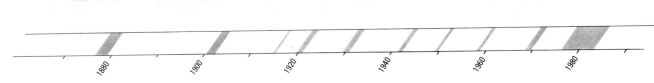

failure (total or partial) of the rains

▽ **Figure 8.9** The effect of drought in Latin America. Failure of rains causes rivers to dry up

The Sertao (an area of north-east Brazil inland from the coast) is said to suffer from periodic drought. This area (Figure 8.11) experiences a savanna climate (page 18) which means that each year it has one wet season (January–June) and one dry season (July–December). It is the total or partial failure of the rains which causes a water shortage, i.e. a drought. As Figure 8.8 shows, the failure of the rains occurs fairly regularly every ten years or so, but since 1976 there have been several successive years of water shortage.

Problems of living in the Sertao

- 80–90 per cent of rain falls in five months, followed by a long dry season (Figure 8.9).
- Periodic crop failure results from 'drought' and the unrealiability of the rainfall.
- Subsistence farmers grow nothing surplus to their needs. Crop failure causes a drop in production (80 per cent drop in 1970).
- Incomes are extremely low.
- The majority are landless or own very small farms (Figure 8.10) because of fragmentation of farms for successive generations.
- Although the population density of the area *appears* to be fairly low, it is nevertheless very high for its resources (page 39).
- Many children (up to 50 per cent) die because of malnutrition.
- The soils are poor – either heavily leached or saline.
- Until recently there has been very little national help.
- In times of drought farmers can either join 'work teams' (building roads or reservoirs) or migrate to urban areas, swelling the shanty towns.

farm size (in hectares)	under 10.0	10.1 to 99.9	over 100
% of total land area	4	26	70
% of total farms	58	34	8
% of total farm labour force	86	12	2

△ **Figure 8.10** Farm sizes in the Sertao

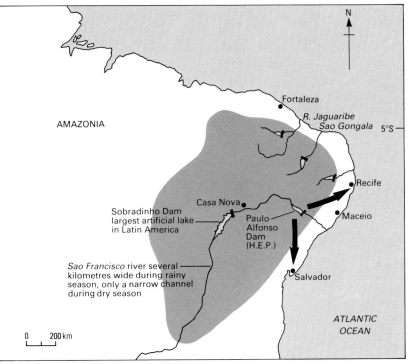

Sertao

reservoirs

H.E.P. sent to Recife and Salvador

What was achieved between 1970 and 1980

- Despite several large reservoirs, only 20 per cent of the planned area was irrigated.
- Of the planned creation of numerous five hectare plots for new farmers only ten per cent had actually been achieved.
- Although production of crops increased it was only 35 per cent of the target.
- There was only a minimal increase in jobs – although more bureaucratic jobs were created in the cities.
- Despite being given money to grow their first crops, many farmers began in debt and have never recovered.
- There was some improvement in health.
- H.E.P. was provided on the Sao Francisco (Figure 8.11).
- There was some employment in building new roads and reservoirs.
- A smaller number than planned had moved to the Amazon Forest (see Chapters 3 and 9).

Why reservoirs were thought to be the answer

- They were the answer in North America.
- More water would increase farmland and provide constant supplies.
- Food supplies would be increased, especially citrus fruits and vegetables for export, so giving a quick return (high value crops).
- Local income levels might be raised by up to five times.
- Local employment would be created – hopefully one job for every 20 hectares of irrigated land.
- Rural depopulation would be prevented or limited (also reducing a problem in urban areas).

Why have reservoir and irrigation schemes not succeeded?

- They were extremely expensive to build for a low economic return.
- Very few jobs were created – the work is not labour intensive.
- Building the reservoirs displaced five times more people (70 000 by the Sobradinho Dam) than it gave jobs to.
- The Sobradinho Dam led to the flooding of the most fertile areas (Figure 8.12).
- Those displaced have not received compensation, causing social unrest; many still moved to urban areas.
- The schemes favoured the already well off, and hardly affected the poorest groups, who remained very poor. Two-thirds of the farmers have never got over the initial debt, and the gap between rich and poor has widened.
- There were insufficient high quality crops and a lack of storage and marketing facilities (200 kilometres from the sea).
- New farmers were only given two weeks' training – no other education or advice. Crops all ripened at the same time.
- One scheme had 300 bureaucrats but only resettled 123 families.
- No attempts were made to improve soil quality.
- The selection process for potential landlords was extremely rigid – each had to be head of a family, aged 19 to 49, a Brazilian who had lived in one place for three years and had had no other job than farming, of good health, with several sons (to work the land in order to reduce hired labour), and of good character.
- Typical of developing countries – any surplus produce was exported and not processed first.

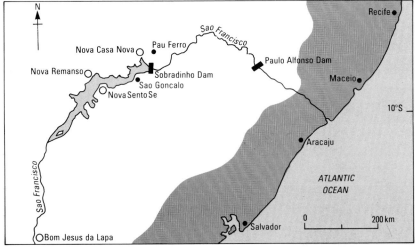

O   re-settlement sites of villages flooded by reservoir

approximate extent of humid coastal zone (remainder of area suffers from water shortage)

△ **Figure 8.12** The Sobradinho Dam

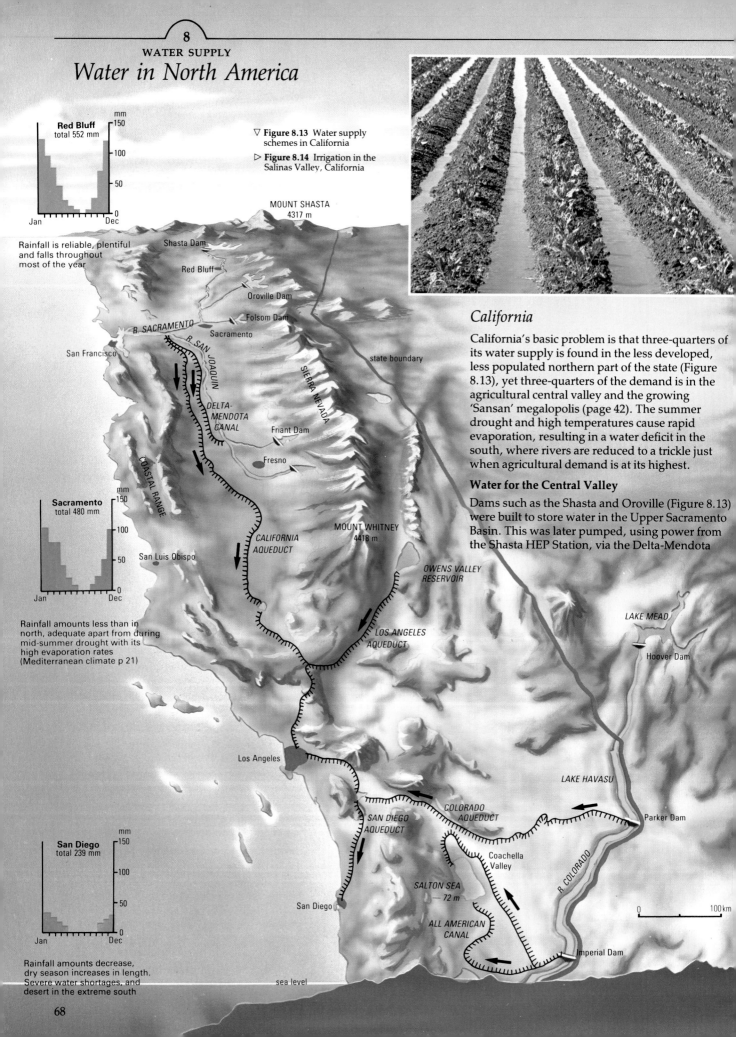

Red Bluff
total 552 mm

Rainfall is reliable, plentiful and falls throughout most of the year

▽ **Figure 8.13** Water supply schemes in California

▷ **Figure 8.14** Irrigation in the Salinas Valley, California

MOUNT SHASTA
4317 m

Shasta Dam

Red Bluff

Oroville Dam

Folsom Dam

R. SACRAMENTO

R. SAN JOAQUIN

Sacramento

San Francisco

state boundary

SIERRA NEVADA

DELTA-MENDOTA CANAL

Friant Dam

Fresno

Sacramento
total 480 mm

San Luis Obispo

COASTAL RANGE

CALIFORNIA AQUEDUCT

MOUNT WHITNEY
4418 m

Rainfall amounts less than in north, adequate apart from during mid-summer drought with its high evaporation rates (Mediterranean climate p 21)

OWENS VALLEY RESERVOIR

LAKE MEAD

Hoover Dam

LOS ANGELES AQUEDUCT

Los Angeles

LAKE HAVASU

San Diego
total 239 mm

SAN DIEGO AQUEDUCT

COLORADO AQUEDUCT

Parker Dam

Coachella Valley

R. COLORADO

San Diego

SALTON SEA
— 72 m

0   100 km

ALL AMERICAN CANAL

Imperial Dam

Rainfall amounts decrease, dry season increases in length. Severe water shortages, and desert in the extreme south

sea level

California

California's basic problem is that three-quarters of its water supply is found in the less developed, less populated northern part of the state (Figure 8.13), yet three-quarters of the demand is in the agricultural central valley and the growing 'Sansan' megalopolis (page 42). The summer drought and high temperatures cause rapid evaporation, resulting in a water deficit in the south, where rivers are reduced to a trickle just when agricultural demand is at its highest.

Water for the Central Valley

Dams such as the Shasta and Oroville (Figure 8.13) were built to store water in the Upper Sacramento Basin. This was later pumped, using power from the Shasta HEP Station, via the Delta-Mendota

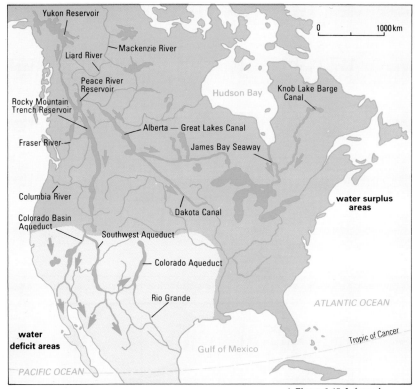

Water for southern California

As the graphs in Figure 8.13 show, rainfall in the Los Angeles–San Diego region is very limited, and falls mainly in the winter season. To satisfy the huge demands of farmers, industrialists and domestic users, water is transferred from the Sacramento Delta, the Owens Valley Reservoir and the Lower Colorado River.

Using Figure 8.13

1 Name the three aqueducts carrying water to Southern California.

2 How long is each of these aqueducts?

3 What problems had to be overcome in building these aqueducts?

4 Could such a scheme have been created in a developing country?

The aqueduct from the Colorado carries enough water for every inhabitant of Los Angeles to use up to 400 litres per day.

Water for the south-east of California

The area around the Salton Sea is known as North America's 'Winter Greenhouse' for, despite its being a desert, temperatures are high enough for crops to grow throughout the year – indeed it is possible to grow two or three crops a year on the same piece of land. To overcome the water shortage, water is pumped from the Colorado via the Coachella and All-American Canals (Figures 8.13 and 8.15).

Supplying water has created problems

□ Loss of water in reservoirs through evaporation increases the salinity of the lake.

□ Water draining back from the fields also adds salt to the water.

□ High temperatures bring salts to the surface.

□ To remove salt from the soil even more fresh water is needed to flush the salt away.

□ To try to reduce salinity, 27 000 kilometres of drainage tiles have been laid. Resting two metres underground, they limit the accumulation of salt at or near the surface.

□ Water extracted from the Sacramento Delta area has caused the ground to subside by several metres, so that parts are below sea level and the risk of flooding has increased.

□ Water flowing into dams brings much silt which will slowly fill in the reservoirs.

□ High construction costs result in high water charges to farmers and so increase the cost of produce.

□ The delta scheme has upset salmon breeding.

Future water transfer plans in North America

Figure 8.16 shows some of the ambitious plans which aim to carry the excess water from northern parts of the continent to the drier south-west, and also to Mexico.

Canal (Figure 8.13) to the upper parts of the San Joaquin Valley which has a low and unreliable flow in summer (despite having its own reservoirs such as the Friant Dam). This water is then used to irrigate the fruit and vegetable farms previously described on page 59. Figure 8.14 shows the intensive land use resulting from irrigation in the Central Valley.

△ **Figure 8.15** Infra-red photograph taken from Apollo 9 over the Colorado River and Salton Sea. Intensive agriculture is made possible by the use of irrigation – this shows up as dark red areas in the photo (top)

△ **Figure 8.16** Proposed water transfer schemes in North America

Types of forest

Equatorial (page 16) This has an evergreen appearance because temperatures and rainfall are high throughout the year and so there is no need for the trees to shed their leaves at a given time. The trees are *hardwoods* (Figure 9.1A) but have had relatively little demand until recently by the developed countries. As a result half of the world's trees are found in these latitudes (Figure 9.2). However, in the last decade rapid clearances have begun (page 71), and considerable concern is expressed for their future.

Tropical deciduous (page 18) are so called because the trees lose their leaves in the hot, dry season. These are less widely distributed than the equatorial (Figure 9.1A), and have been cleared for fuel and farming.

Sub-tropical broad-leaved evergreen (page 21) are found in areas with a Mediterranean climate. The leaves are waxy and leathery to limit transpiration. Again, most trees have been cleared for farming.

Temperate deciduous and mixed forests (page 23) These used to cover most of lowland USA (Figure 9.1B) but have been cleared for farming, for producing charcoal for industry, and for urban growth. The deciduous trees lose their leaves during the cold winter season.

Boreal forests (page 25) These consist of vast stands of coniferous (evergreen) trees (Figure 9.1B). These trees are in large demand in the developed world for timber, pulp and paper. They still account for a quarter of the world's forests in the 1980s for, despite their extensive exploitation, much afforestation also takes place (Figure 9.2).

▽ **Figure 9.1** Forest resources in the Americas

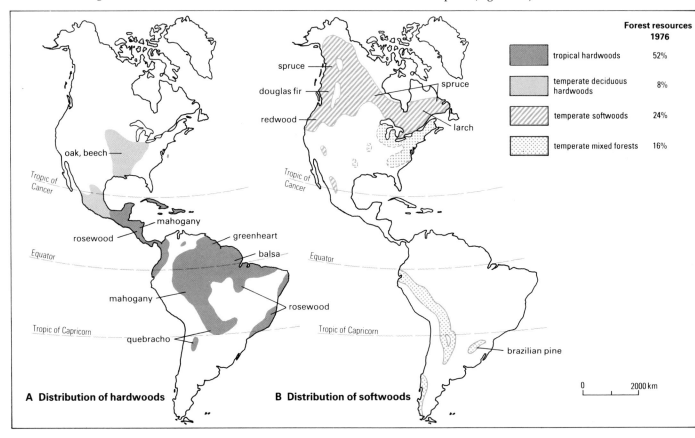

Forest resources 1976	
tropical hardwoods	52%
temperate deciduous hardwoods	8%
temperate softwoods	24%
temperate mixed forests	16%

A Distribution of hardwoods

B Distribution of softwoods

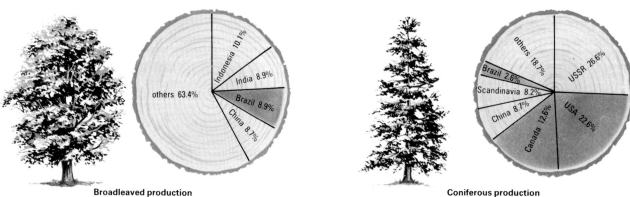

Broadleaved production

Coniferous production

Timber production 1980

◁ **Figure 9.2** World timber production

Forestry in the developing world

The recent rapid deforestation of tropical forests has become a major issue of world concern. At times pilots flying over these areas have to fly blind because of the smoke of burning trees. Clearances are taking place because of:

- The needs of shifting cultivators (pages 52–3), who comprise one-ninth of the world's population, trying to grow sufficient food for their survival (Figure 9.3).
- The growing population rates of most developed countries (Figure 4.5), demanding more land for food and housing.
- The needs of less developed countries to use wood as their major source of fuel (pages 74–5).
- Highway construction (Chapter 13).

△ **Figure 9.3** Forest clearance in the Amazon Basin

◁ **Figure 9.4** Timber being transported from Ilanos to Bogota, Colombia

▽ **Figure 9.5** Report from 1982 Conference Proposals on the Future of the Tropical Rainforests

- Attempts to resettle many of Latin America's landless. In Brazil 70 per cent of the population are landless, and the government has recently tried to resettle people from the dry north-east of their country (pages 66 and 67). Yet farming is difficult because of the heavy leaching and soil erosion follows deforestation (page 17).

In Brazil 38 per cent of the clearances are for ranching and agriculture, 32 per cent for small-scale farming and fuel, 26 per cent for highways, and 4 per cent for timber.

Rates of Clearance

It is estimated that 14 hectares of tropical forest are being cleared every minute, and in Brazil alone an area the size of Wales is cleared every year (Figure 9.4). Parts of Central America lost 75 per cent of their trees between 1975 and 1980, and one fifth of Amazonia has been cleared since 1960. UNO anticipates that at present rates of clearance, the tropical forests will have gone by A.D. 2020 – and the alarming consequences of this are explained on pages 118–19. A recent conference on tropical forests made the recommendations listed in Figure 9.5.

At least 10 per cent of the world's tropical rain forests should be set aside as conservation areas, with effective protection monitoring and research. At present only 2 per cent is conserved.

Two hundred and fifty million farmers in the tropics are directly dependent on the forest for their livelihood. They need help to use the resource on a long term basis. Public education for all those dependent on the forest should be increased substantially to explain its value for their continued welfare.

There should be greater control of forest clearance on lands unsuitable for permanent agriculture and the encouragement of more efficient use of land already cleared. Pressure on natural forest can be reduced by providing tree plantations of fuel-wood, pulpwood and commercial timber.

Developed countries have as great an economic stake in the long term survival of tropical rain forests as do the countries in which the forests grow. Developed nations should, therefore, consider assuming a much larger share of the costs of conserving this habitat. For example, market prices of tropical forest wood must rise to reflect the real value of these products. Developed nations should provide increased training programmes in tropical ecology and management.

The symposium delegates felt that the fate of tropical rain forests has become of vital interest to people everywhere. Conservation of the forests should illustrate the concept of one world, indivisible in its interactions and responsibilities.

Forestry in Canada

Location and types

The boreal forests stretch across the continent in an unbroken belt 500 to 2100 km wide (Figure 9.1B). The coniferous trees have become adapted to the long, cold winters (page 25). East of the Rockies, spruce, larch and hemlock dominate but take up to 100 years to mature (twice as long as similar species in Scotland). West of the Rockies, in British Columbia, where the climate is milder and wetter, large Douglas firs dominate. These grow up to 60 metres in height, and exceed 2 metres in diameter. This area contains less than 2 per cent of Canada's forest area, but supplies over 25 per cent of its cut timber.

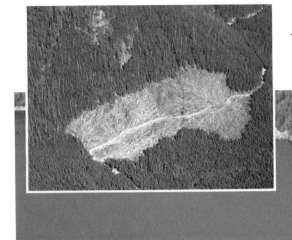

◁ **Figure 9.7** Deforestation scars, British Columbia. Logging companies plant seedlings to replace harvested trees.

△ **Figure 9.6** Mechanised harvesting equipment in British Columbia

How important are these forests?

- ☐ One in every ten Canadians gains employment by working in the forests or dealing with forest products.
- ☐ Pulp and paper are Canada's second most important export, and the country is the world's second major exporter.
- ☐ They provide areas for recreation and wild life.

Lumbering

Lumbering is now highly mechanised (Figure 9.6). The trees are felled by chainsaws and are then dragged to roads by skidders or carried by sky-line winches. From there large vehicles can lift up the trunks and remove them from the forest. Each year thousands of hectares are cleared (Figure 9.7), and many more are destroyed by fire (Figure 9.8) and disease. In the early days of lumbering, trees were felled and not replaced – a so-called 'robber economy'. Today forests are treated as a 'crop', and cleared areas are renewed.

▷ **Figure 9.8** Forest fire fighting, Quebec

Figure 9.9 (Main picture) Logs being towed across a lake, British Colombia

Aims of the Provincial Forest Services

☐ Developing areas of afforestation for the future supply of timber and timber products. It takes 100 years and 15 trees on the Canadian Shield to produce one tonne of newsprint.

☐ Maintaining an adequate supply of high quality trees. The forest services determine how much timber should be cut and what size of tree should be felled. The sustained yield policy states that if a new forest area takes 100 years to mature, then only one-tenth of that forest should be cleared and replanted each year in a ten-year cycle.

☐ Maintaining sufficient trees to protect the environment by reducing rapid run-off after heavy rainfall and snow melt, which in turn could cause soil erosion, flooding and the silting of lakes and reservoirs. Afforestation also reduces the scars shown in Figure 9.7.

☐ Controlling forest diseases and pests.

☐ Providing fire protection.

☐ Providing tourist, recreational and sporting facilities. Many parts of Canada's forests have picnic and camping areas.

☐ Protecting wild life.

The movement of timber

Much of this is still done via the lakes and rivers. The trees, on reaching one of the many lakes, are tied together in log rafts and towed. The rafts are kept together by an outer rim or boom (Figure 9.9). Problems in transportation are caused by the freezing of the lakes in winter, by the difficulties of getting from one lake to another, especially since the lakes are often separated by rapids, and by obstructions caused by the building of HEP stations. When the trees reach a sawmill or a pulp and paper mill, propellers submerged near the shore suck them under the boom (Figure 9.10) and into the mill. Gates in the boom allow access for ships.

Uses of Canada's timber

Most is used for pulp and paper (Figure 9.11), plywood and veneer, timber and furniture.

Location of sawmills and pulp and papermills

These are usually lakeside sites, or better still on such navigable seaways as the St Lawrence, near to an HEP station which provides the electricity, and as near to the workforce and a market as possible. Ideal sites are in British Columbia (export to Japan) and along the St Lawrence (export to Western Europe).

▷ **Figure 9.10** Log sorting at Port Alberni, British Columbia

▷ **Figure 9.11** Pulp mill and log booms at Vancouver (far right)

◁ **Figure 10.2** Developing the Alaskan oilfields necessitate the building of a pipeline to transport the oil to the ice-free port of Valdez

△ **Figure 10.3** Brazilian woma collecting wood

One of the greatest differences between developed and developing countries is the contrast in the amount of energy each uses. The 'developed' countries use, per capita, over 15 times more coal, oil and gas than the developing countries. These differences are given in Figure 10.1. Notice the special vertical scale. It is a logarithmic scale, which is needed because of the great contrast in figures between the developed and developing countries. The *actual* figures are given in brackets to try to help you to understand the graph. Using Figure 10.1 –

1 What is the GNP for (*a*) the USA (*b*) Uruguay (*c*) Brazil?

2 How much energy is used per capita in (*a*) USA (*b*) Uruguay (*c*) Brazil?

3 Can you explain any possible relationship between GNP and energy consumption between North America (a developed continent) and Latin America (a developing continent)?

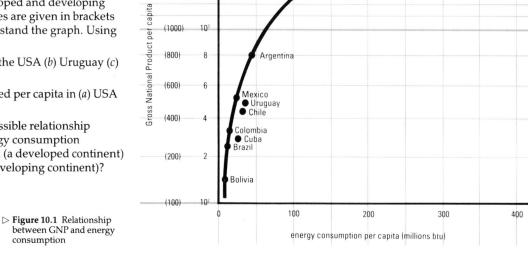

▷ **Figure 10.1** Relationship between GNP and energy consumption

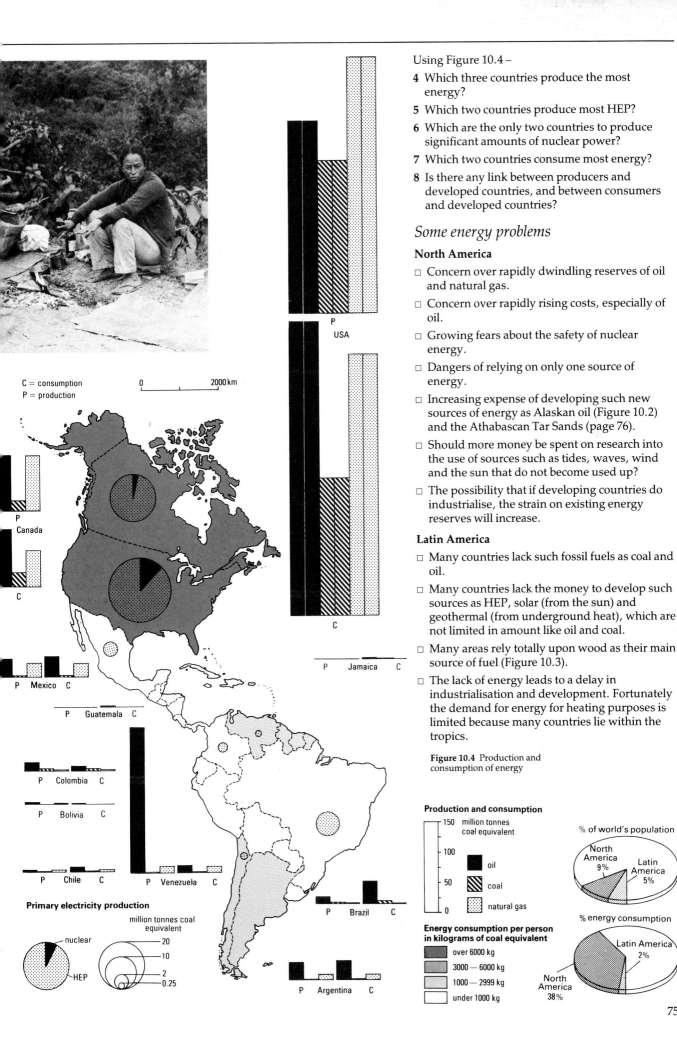

Using Figure 10.4 –

4 Which three countries produce the most energy?

5 Which two countries produce most HEP?

6 Which are the only two countries to produce significant amounts of nuclear power?

7 Which two countries consume most energy?

8 Is there any link between producers and developed countries, and between consumers and developed countries?

Some energy problems

North America

☐ Concern over rapidly dwindling reserves of oil and natural gas.

☐ Concern over rapidly rising costs, especially of oil.

☐ Growing fears about the safety of nuclear energy.

☐ Dangers of relying on only one source of energy.

☐ Increasing expense of developing such new sources of energy as Alaskan oil (Figure 10.2) and the Athabascan Tar Sands (page 76).

☐ Should more money be spent on research into the use of sources such as tides, waves, wind and the sun that do not become used up?

☐ The possibility that if developing countries do industrialise, the strain on existing energy reserves will increase.

Latin America

☐ Many countries lack such fossil fuels as coal and oil.

☐ Many countries lack the money to develop such sources as HEP, solar (from the sun) and geothermal (from underground heat), which are not limited in amount like oil and coal.

☐ Many areas rely totally upon wood as their main source of fuel (Figure 10.3).

☐ The lack of energy leads to a delay in industrialisation and development. Fortunately the demand for energy for heating purposes is limited because many countries lie within the tropics.

Figure 10.4 Production and consumption of energy

Production and consumption

150 million tonnes coal equivalent

100

■ oil

50

▨ coal

0

▦ natural gas

% of world's population

North America 9%
Latin America 5%

% energy consumption

Latin America 2%

North America 38%

Primary electricity production

million tonnes coal equivalent

nuclear

HEP

20
10
2
0.25

Energy consumption per person in kilograms of coal equivalent

over 6000 kg

3000 — 6000 kg

1000 — 2999 kg

under 1000 kg

C = consumption
P = production

0   2000 km

P USA

P Canada

C

P Mexico C

P Guatemala C

P Colombia C

P Bolivia C

P Chile C

P Venezuela C

P Brazil C

P Argentina C

P Jamaica C

75

Oil and natural gas

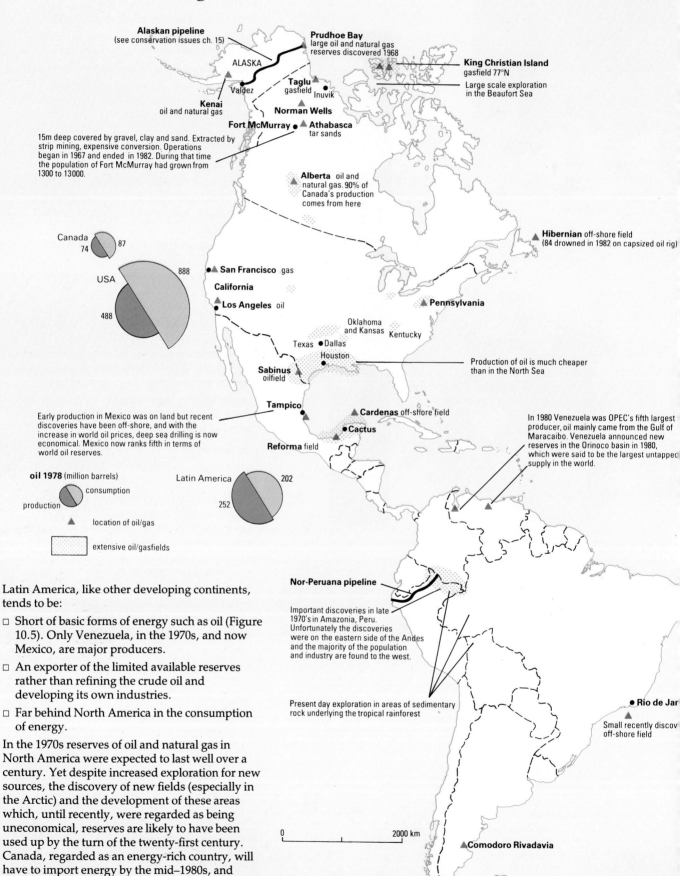

Alaskan pipeline
(see conservation issues ch. 15)

ALASKA

Valdez

Kenai
oil and natural gas

Prudhoe Bay
large oil and natural gas
reserves discovered 1968

King Christian Island
gasfield 77°N

Large scale exploration
in the Beaufort Sea

Taglu
gasfield   Inuvik

Norman Wells

Fort McMurray ● ▲ **Athabasca**
tar sands

15m deep covered by gravel, clay and sand. Extracted by
strip mining, expensive conversion. Operations
began in 1967 and ended in 1982. During that time
the population of Fort McMurray had grown from
1300 to 13000.

Alberta oil and
natural gas. 90% of
Canada's production
comes from here

Hibernian off-shore field
(84 drowned in 1982 on capsized oil rig)

Canada
74   87

● ▲ **San Francisco** gas

California

USA

488   888

▲ **Los Angeles** oil

Pennsylvania

Oklahoma
and Kansas   Kentucky

Texas ● Dallas
Houston ●

Sabinus
oilfield

Production of oil is much cheaper
than in the North Sea

Tampico

▲ **Cardenas** off-shore field

● **Cactus**

Early production in Mexico was on land but recent
discoveries have been off-shore, and with the
increase in world oil prices, deep sea drilling is now
economical. Mexico now ranks fifth in terms of
world oil reserves.

Reforma field

In 1980 Venezuela was OPEC's fifth largest
producer, oil mainly came from the Gulf of
Maracaibo. Venezuela announced new
reserves in the Orinoco basin in 1980,
which were said to be the largest untapped
supply in the world.

oil 1978 (million barrels)

consumption

production

▲ location of oil/gas

extensive oil/gasfields

Latin America
252   202

Nor-Peruana pipeline

Important discoveries in late
1970's in Amazonia, Peru.
Unfortunately the discoveries
were on the eastern side of the Andes
and the majority of the population
and industry are found to the west.

Present day exploration in areas of sedimentary
rock underlying the tropical rainforest

● **Rio de Jar**

▲ Small recently discov
off-shore field

0 ———— 2000 km

▲ **Comodoro Rivadavia**

Latin America, like other developing continents,
tends to be:

☐ Short of basic forms of energy such as oil (Figure
10.5). Only Venezuela, in the 1970s, and now
Mexico, are major producers.

☐ An exporter of the limited available reserves
rather than refining the crude oil and
developing its own industries.

☐ Far behind North America in the consumption
of energy.

In the 1970s reserves of oil and natural gas in
North America were expected to last well over a
century. Yet despite increased exploration for new
sources, the discovery of new fields (especially in
the Arctic) and the development of these areas
which, until recently, were regarded as being
uneconomical, reserves are likely to have been
used up by the turn of the twenty-first century.
Canada, regarded as an energy-rich country, will
have to import energy by the mid–1980s, and
could have used up all her oil and natural gas by
the mid-1990s.

Figure 10.5 Oil and natural
gas producing areas

Gas and oil reserves around the Falkland Islands could le
further disputes between Britain and Argentina

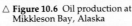

△ **Figure 10.6** Oil production at Mikkleson Bay, Alaska

Figure 10.7 Oil exploration in the rain forest (top right)

▷ **Figure 10.8** Off-shore oil production; working on the rig 30 metres above the drilling floor

Problems of exploring new areas and exploiting new reserves

1 Figure 10.6 shows an oil-rig in Alaska. Can you suggest four reasons why exploration is difficult in these latitudes?

2 Figure 10.7 is in the Amazon forest of Peru. Can you suggest four different reasons why exploration here is restricted?

3 Figure 10.8 is one of many off-shore oil rigs around the Americas. What difficulties have to be faced in these areas? Why is so much present exploration taking place off-shore and why is it less economic to do so?

The presence of oil does not always mean successful development

☐ In Athabasca oil seeps into porous rock but the costs of extracting it have become too great (Figure 10.5).

☐ Mexico, which in the 1920s was the second producer of oil in the world after the USA, has recently discovered large off-shore fields (Figure 10.5). Although Mexico tried not to export all this oil, and tried to develop industries, the so-called 'bonanza' did not avert virtual bankruptcy in 1982.

Coal and nuclear power

Coal

Figure 10.9 shows the possible recoverable coal deposits. Which country has the largest reserves? Which continent appears to have no worthwhile reserves? (In fact it has less than 1 per cent.) How has this affected industrial development in the Americas?

Coal in the USA

From a peak of 630 million tonnes in 1947, production fell to only 405 million tonnes in 1961, since when it recovered to reach an all-time high of 772 million tonnes in 1979. 'King Coal' has regained its supremacy mainly because of foreign oil disruptions, higher oil prices, dwindling world supplies of oil and natural gas, and new coalmining technology.

The distribution of coalfields is shown in Figure 10.10. The largest and oldest area is in the Appalachians, the youngest and most rapidly growing areas are in the west.

Why the western fields have gained at the expense of the eastern fields since 1960

☐ The Appalachian fields have been long established, and now suffer from exhaustion or from rising mining costs as seams get more difficult to reach.

☐ The Clean Air Act of 1970 imposed severe restrictions upon the sulphur content which could be released into the atmosphere when coal was burnt. Figures 10.10 and 10.11 show that the western fields produce coal of a much lower sulphur content.

☐ There has been a rapid increase in 'opencast' or 'strip' mining (Figure 10.12). Large machines can produce far more coal per day (27 tonnes per man) than can underground mines (14 tonnes per man in 1978) (Figure 10.13).

☐ The cost of labour has increased, together with uncertainties in labour relations, in the eastern fields.

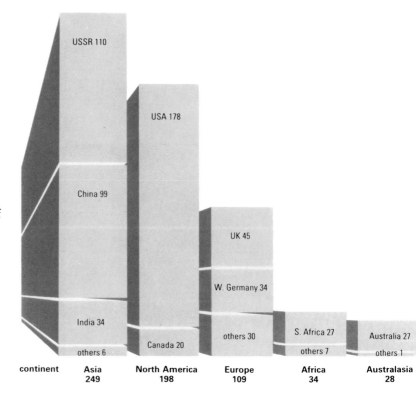

△ **Figure 10.9** Economically recoverable coal deposits, 1980 (in millions of tonnes)

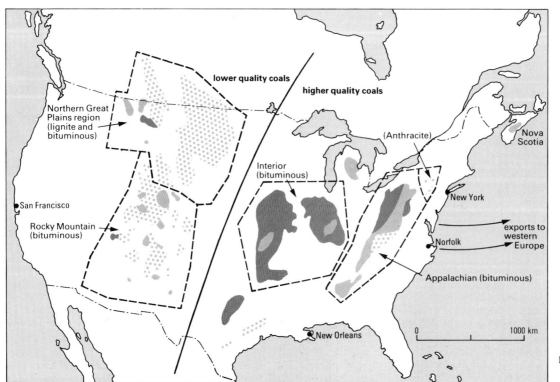

◁ **Figure 10.10** North American coal producing areas

% sulphur content by weight

- less than 1
- 1–3
- more than 3
- --- boundary of coal producing area

▷ **Figure 10.14** Nuclear power station at Three Mile Island, Pennsylvania

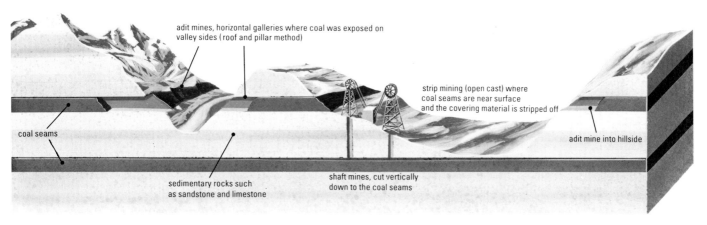

adit mines, horizontal galleries where coal was exposed on valley sides (roof and pillar method)

coal seams

sedimentary rocks such as sandstone and limestone

shaft mines, cut vertically down to the coal seams

strip mining (open cast) where coal seams are near surface and the covering material is stripped off

adit mine into hillside

▽ **Figure 10.11** Characteristics of US coal producing areas

△ **Figure 10.12** Different types of coal mining

▽ **Figure 10.13** Mechanised strip mining in Eastern Montana

	West	**Interior**	**Appalachia**
sulphur content	80% under 1% SO_2	Average 5% SO_2	Only 23% under 5% SO_2
calorific value	low	medium/high	high
coal type	sub-bituminous plus bituminous and lignite	bituminous and sub-bituminous	bituminous and anthracite
% open cast mining	90%	65%	45%
use	steam	steam & coke	steam, coke & other
transport	still being developed- mainly rail	already developed- rail & water	already developed- rail & water
employment 1975	9020	29 150	151 720
no. of pits 1975	103	372	5693
production m.tons 1979	203	162 (1975) (1979 N.A.)	464
reserves	large reserves low sulphur	medium reserves high sulphur	medium reserves highest sulphur
history of coal area	new	established	long established

Yet the west has disadvantages

☐ Although the largest reserves are now in the west, peak demand is in the east. The transportation of coal adds 60 per cent to its cost.

☐ Strip mining in the scenic and farming areas of the west causes opposition from conservationists and farmers.

☐ Although the coal is low in sulphur content, it also has a low calorific value (Figure 10.11). This means it is less effective for heating than coals found in the east – and so more coal is needed to produce the same amount of energy.

☐ The conversion of coal into gas needs vast quantities of water, and water is precious in this increasingly arid area.

Nuclear power

The 1950s and 1960s saw North America turning increasingly towards nuclear power as its long-term solution to obtaining 'plentiful, cheap electricity'. Nuclear power has many advantages and disadvantages. By 1979 there were 72 power stations operative in the USA – mainly in the energy-short areas of New England, the south-east and California. Many more were planned, but expansion has been delayed following the Three Mile Island (Figure 10.14) accident when radioactivity leaked into the atmosphere and many people had to be evacuated for a time.

79

Water power

Hydro-electric power (HEP)

HEP has the advantages of being clean, renewable and, once over the high initial cost of construction, providing power relatively cheaply.

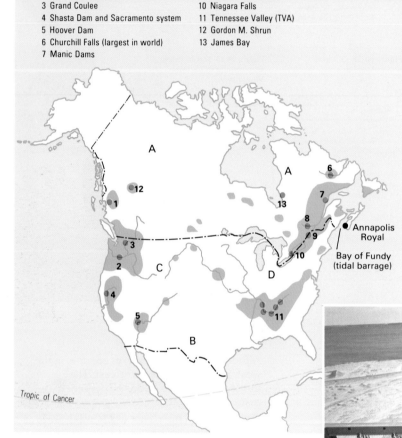

▽ **Figure 10.15** HEP in North America

HEP producing areas

●1 major HEP schemes

A non-producing areas

1 Kemano (for Kitimat)
2 Bonneville Dam
3 Grand Coulee
4 Shasta Dam and Sacramento system
5 Hoover Dam
6 Churchill Falls (largest in world)
7 Manic Dams
8 Saguenay system
9 St Lawrence system
10 Niagara Falls
11 Tennessee Valley (TVA)
12 Gordon M. Shrun
13 James Bay

0   1000km

Annapolis Royal

Bay of Fundy (tidal barrage)

Tropic of Cancer

The ideal site for an HEP station

☐ Heavy, reliable rainfall evenly distributed throughout the year to give a constant run-off and to maintain an even river flow.

☐ A steep gradient to provide a good 'head' or fall of water.

☐ Natural lakes (or man-made reservoirs) to store water to regulate the flow to the turbines in the power station.

☐ A large drainage basin to trap sufficient water.

☐ Narrow, steep-sided valleys for the building of dams.

☐ A relatively near market for electricity, because electricity loses its energy if it is transported over long distances.

The locations of the major areas for HEP in North America are shown in Figure 10.15. This map also shows four areas labelled A to D where HEP has not been developed for one of the following reasons:

☐ Insufficient water supply due to a desert climate.

☐ A coal mining area giving a rival source of power.

☐ Water stored for most of the year as snow or ice.

☐ A mountainous area but too isolated from large markets.

Fit each of these four statements to one of the letters A to D.

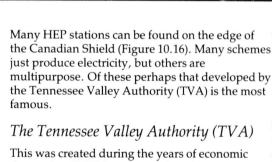

Figure 10.16 HEP station in the James Bay area (interior and exterior)

Many HEP stations can be found on the edge of the Canadian Shield (Figure 10.16). Many schemes just produce electricity, but others are multipurpose. Of these perhaps that developed by the Tennessee Valley Authority (TVA) is the most famous.

The Tennessee Valley Authority (TVA)

This was created during the years of economic depression (1933) in an area where incomes were less than half the national average, rivers frequently flooded, overcultivation had led to severe soil erosion, there was no industry, and only three per cent of homes had electricity, and which was suffering from rural overpopulation (not unlike many areas of Latin America in the 1980s).

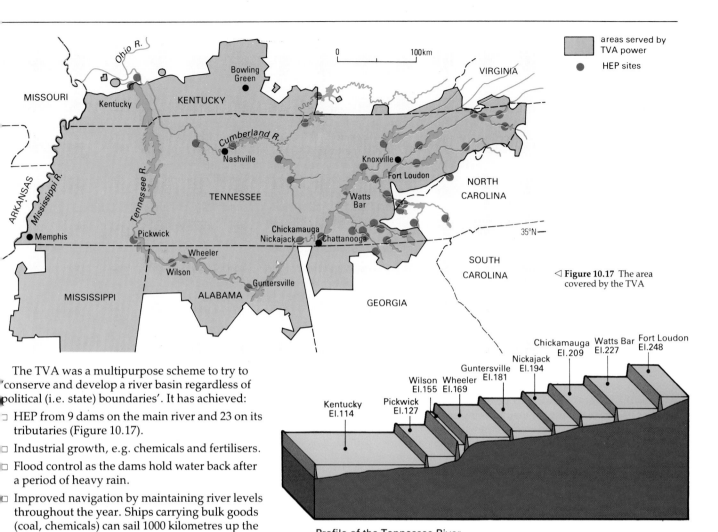

◁ **Figure 10.17** The area covered by the TVA

Profile of the Tennessee River
All elevations are in metres above sea level

The TVA was a multipurpose scheme to try to 'conserve and develop a river basin regardless of political (i.e. state) boundaries'. It has achieved:

- HEP from 9 dams on the main river and 23 on its tributaries (Figure 10.17).

- Industrial growth, e.g. chemicals and fertilisers.

- Flood control as the dams hold water back after a period of heavy rain.

- Improved navigation by maintaining river levels throughout the year. Ships carrying bulk goods (coal, chemicals) can sail 1000 kilometres up the main river.

- Improved farming by reducing soil erosion, and allowing diversified crops and animals.

- Improved water supply for domestic use and farming.

- Afforestation, which reduces run-off and flooding.

- Tourism on the newly created reservoirs and in the forests.

- Improved health by draining swampy areas and so finally eradicating malaria.

- A much improved standard of living.

Could such a project not be applied to Latin American countries? Give reasons for your answer.

Tidal power

The world's first tidal power station was opened at La Rance in France in 1966. The success of this station stimulated interest in eastern Canada where, in the Bay of Fundy (Figure 10.15), the largest tidal ranges in the world occur – a range as high as 16 metres on spring tides.

An initial report concluded that while tidal energy generation was possible, it was not economically viable, because at that time other forms of energy, especially oil, were much cheaper. Since oil and coal prices rose in the 1970s and nuclear power has not fulfilled its earlier promise, the price of tidal power is now much more competitive. As a result Nova Scotia has constructed a pilot plant at Annapolis Royal on the Bay of Fundy (Figure 10.18), and this was opened in 1983.

Like HEP tidal power is clean and renewable, but the initital construction costs are very high.

△ **Figure 10.18** Bay of Fundy tidal barrage

Energy for Latin America

Wood for fuel

The majority of people living in the developing world depend upon firewood to cook their daily food. A report published in 1980 estimated that 101 million people in the world could not find enough firewood to meet their basic needs. On average each inhabitant in the developing world uses one ton of firewood a year, which is about 2.75 kg, or a few thickish sticks, per day. Yet as more firewood is consumed, families have to spend more time and walk further each day to collect just enough wood for their cooking and heating (Figure 10.3).

The World Bank, which has named the Andean Region and the Caribbean coast of Central America as two of the four worst areas for lack of firewood, claims that the developing countries need to plant 50 million hectares by A.D. 2000 just to meet the demand for wood for fuel.

The use of trees for firewood can lead to a loss of treecrops previously used for food, a loss of shade for younger trees, and an increase in soil erosion. Also, as the supply of firewood decreases, poorer families use animal dung for their fires instead of spreading it over their fields, an action which can lead to a reduction in the often already low crop yields. If only the vast areas of tropical rainforest being burnt to make room for cattle ranches could be used for firewood!

Wood used as fuel is likely to be the only source of energy for domestic use and village industry in many developing world countries until well into the next century. It is essential therefore that more countries carry out a major tree planting campaign immediately, otherwise the 101 million people mentioned earlier as being short of firewood in the world in 1980 will have increased to 2770 million by A.D. 2000.

Solar power (Figure 10.19)

Those parts of the world which receive most amounts of sunlight tend to correspond with those tropical areas which are in greatest need of energy supplies.

☐ Solar water pumps are being funded by the World Bank to provide cleaner and more reliable water supplies.

☐ Solar refrigerators are being tested in Peru, the Dominican Republic, Haiti, Guatemala, Ecuador and Guyana. These will be used to cool vaccines in remote areas which lack electricity.

▽ **Figure 10.19** Solar powered water heaters like this one at Cape Canaveral need to be introduced in Latin America to make use of expendable, inexhaustible sources of energy

Biomass

An ambitious programme is under way in Brazil to try to rescue that country from its overwhelming dependence upon an oil-based economy, especially in view of the fact that most of the oil has to be imported and at a high cost. In 1982 the state government of Pernambuco in north-east Brazil signed a contract with a private industrial group (Votorantim) to make PVC (polyvinylchloride) from sugar cane. This PVC programme is just one example of the way in which chemicals can be produced from alcohol extracted from plants. By 1985 Brazil hopes to meet at least one-third of her fuel needs from sugar cane.

The key word in this plant–alcohol chain is *biomass*, a term used to describe living vegetable matter from which energy can be obtained. Plants convert solar energy into a chemical form through photosynthesis. Brazilians call this 'energy farming'. Sugar cane gives the best energy yield, but other crops such as cassava, sweet potato, and sorghum are also being tested. One tonne of sugar cane gives between 65 and 70 litres of alcohol – and the 'crop' can be grown over and over again.

As Figure 10.20 shows, the major use of this new form of energy is for cars. Today every second car in Brazil is operated by 'gasohol', a mixture of gasoline (petrol) and alcohol. Conventional cars can use this mixture, though at a reduced efficiency, provided the alcohol content is under 20 per cent.

△ **Figure 10.20** Cars fill up with gasohol in Rio de Janeiro

▽ **Figure 10.21** Geothermal wells, Monitombo volcano, Nicaragua. The generator plant was opened in late 1983 to supply 20% of Nicaragua's electricity needs

Geothermal power One hope for the future of several Andean and Central American states is the development of geothermal power. Water can be pumped down into the earth's crust where it is heated by contact with 'hot rocks', of which there are many in this volcanic area (Figure 10.21). The major problems are in developing this new technology, and the cost which it entails.

Copper mining in Chile

In 1980 Chile was the world's third largest producer of copper, and copper accounted for 48 per cent of Chile's exports. It is mined at Chuquicamata (Figure 11.2).

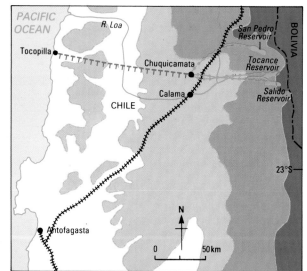
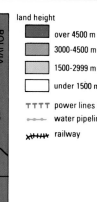

Mining difficulties at Chuquicamata
(Figure 11.2)

☐ The mine lies in the foothills of the rugged Andes mountains (3000 metres). The difficult terrain increases the costs of constructing buildings and communications and of bringing supplies and exporting the copper ore (Figure 11.1).

☐ The distance from the coast, and especially a deep-water harbour, is a problem because virtually all of the copper is exported overseas (and nearly all to the USA). The port of Antofagasta is 250 kilometres away by rail.

☐ Lying in the Atacama Desert, this area receives less than 25 mm of rain per year. The surrounding area is underdeveloped and barren. However, rainfall in the higher Andes to the east is sufficient to create the Rio Loa, which provides a water supply for the mining community and also for the smelting works. There are now three water supplies:

1 Tocance Reservoir (Figure 11.1) on the Rio Loa which provides high quality water for domestic use via a 96-kilometre pipeline.

2 & 3 The San Pedro and the Salido Reservoirs (both on tributaries of the Rio Loa), which tend to be brackish but are piped for use in the mining process and the smelting works.

Again the cost of building these pipelines has been high.

☐ Electricity is also essential, and this is sent through power lines (Figure 11.1) from Tocopilla on the Pacific Coast. However, the construction of the oil-fired power station and the 150 kilometres of transmission lines has also added to the costs of the industry.

☐ The barren nature of the countryside does not encourage the immigration of labour – be it skilled or unskilled.

☐ The desert climate means that all fresh vegetables, fruit and milk have to be 'imported'.

☐ The size and cost of mining operations mean that financial aid from overseas has been essential. The Anaconda Mining Corporation which developed Chuquicamata (Figure 11.2) provided money and equipment; but although their operations provided some work for the Chileans, the bulk of the earnings and profits went to the USA, and little remains within Chile for it to try to develop new industries in an effort to raise its standard of living. The mines were nationalised in 1971, which means that now over half the profits remain in Chile.

☐ The political future is uncertain, because parts of northern Chile are claimed by Peru and Bolivia.

☐ The operation relies on the USA, which is the major market for the copper. There are dangers to any developing country which relies upon one main product for export, and one main overseas market.

△ **Figure 11.1** Location of Chuquicamata

△ **Figure 11.2** Open strip mining of copper at Chuquicamata

Mining in Bolivia and Canada

Tin mining in Bolivia (Figure 11.4)

Tin is found in veins of rock on the Altiplano. Bolivia produces 35 per cent of the world's total (the mines at Llallagua produce 6 per cent).

☐ Most mines are at a height of 4000–5000 metres in very rugged terrain and with a cool climate (Figure 11.3).

☐ This height causes mountain sickness, which results from the lack of oxygen at altitude. The Amerindians have adapted to this by having larger rib cages and lungs (to hold more air) and a modified blood structure.

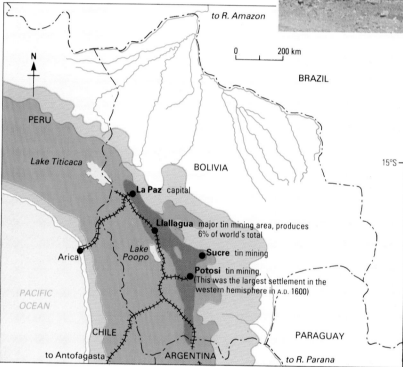

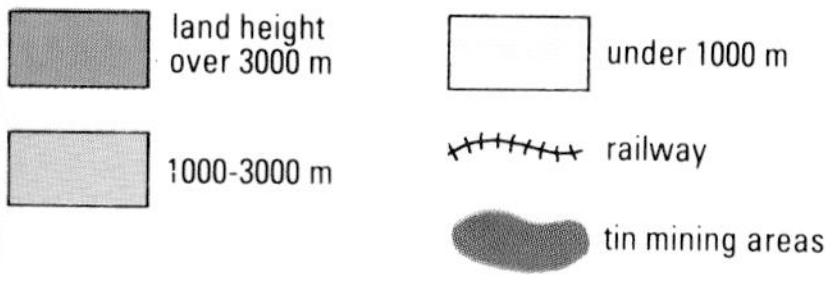

☐ Despite being in the Andes, the area is in the rainshadow of the Western Cordillera, and suffers water shortages and even a winter drought.

☐ Bolivia is land-locked, which means that she has no port of her own. This adds to the already considerable transport problems resulting from the mountains.

☐ Many communities are isolated.

☐ The mines are now very deep. Working at depths of several hundred metres causes problems of high temperatures, lack of ventilation, flooding and lung diseases.

☐ Exhaustion of the better quality and higher grade ores has led to increased production costs.

Mining on the Canadian Shield

The difficulties here include (Figure 11.5):

☐ The long and severe winters (pages 25–6).

☐ The presence, in the north, of areas of permafrost (Figure 2.27) which makes mining difficult.

☐ The large expanses in the south of coniferous forest which must be cleared, and of bare rock, lakes and muskeg (swamp) in the north.

☐ The long, dark winter nights, separated by only a few hours of daylight (and at times none at all within the Arctic circle).

☐ The many lakes, which hinder communications.

☐ The high cost of providing communications, such as the 600-kilometre railway built to connect the iron ore mines of Schefferville with the port of Sept-Iles, and the line, more than 700 kilometres long, recently built to connect the 'new' mining centres of Thompson and Pine Point to the industrial areas or to ports.

☐ The isolation, which tends to cause a rapid turnover of labour.

△ **Figure 11.3** (top right) Siglo Veinte – a tin mining village in Bolivia

△ **Figure 11.4** Location of tin mining in Bolivia

▽ **Figure 11.5** The Canadian Shield

land height over 3000 m

1000-3000 m

under 1000 m

railway

tin mining areas

Mineral wealth

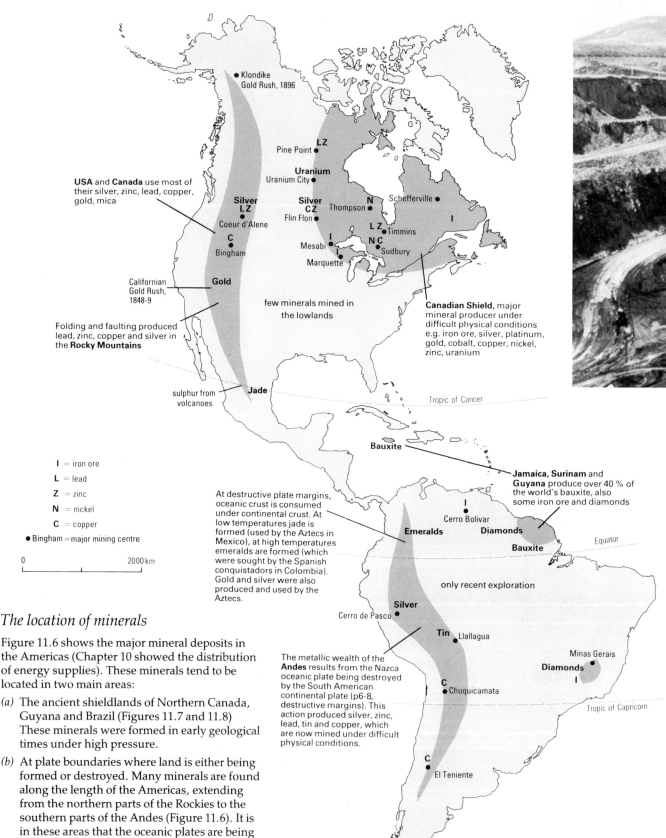

Figure 11.6 Mineral deposits in the Americas

Labels on the map:

USA and Canada use most of their silver, zinc, lead, copper, gold, mica

Klondike Gold Rush, 1896

LZ Pine Point

Uranium — Uranium City

Silver LZ Coeur d'Alene

C Bingham

Silver CZ Flin Flon

Thompson — N

Schefferville

I

N C Sudbury

LZ Timmins

Mesabi — I

Marquette — I

Californian Gold Rush, 1848–9

Gold

Folding and faulting produced lead, zinc, copper and silver in the **Rocky Mountains**

few minerals mined in the lowlands

Canadian Shield, major mineral producer under difficult physical conditions e.g. iron ore, silver, platinum, gold, cobalt, copper, nickel, zinc, uranium

sulphur from volcanoes

Jade

Tropic of Cancer

Bauxite

Jamaica, Surinam and **Guyana** produce over 40 % of the world's bauxite, also some iron ore and diamonds

At destructive plate margins, oceanic crust is consumed under continental crust. At low temperatures jade is formed (used by the Aztecs in Mexico), at high temperatures emeralds are formed (which were sought by the Spanish conquistadors in Colombia). Gold and silver were also produced and used by the Aztecs.

Emeralds

Cerro Bolivar — I

Diamonds

Bauxite

Equator

only recent exploration

Silver — Cerro de Pasco

Tin — Llallagua

The metallic wealth of the **Andes** results from the Nazca oceanic plate being destroyed by the South American continental plate (p6-8, destructive margins). This action produced silver, zinc, lead, tin and copper, which are now mined under difficult physical conditions.

Minas Gerais

Diamonds

I

C Chuquicamata

Tropic of Capricorn

C El Teniente

Legend:

I = iron ore
L = lead
Z = zinc
N = nickel
C = copper
● Bingham = major mining centre

0 ———— 2000 km

The location of minerals

Figure 11.6 shows the major mineral deposits in the Americas (Chapter 10 showed the distribution of energy supplies). These minerals tend to be located in two main areas:

(a) The ancient shieldlands of Northern Canada, Guyana and Brazil (Figures 11.7 and 11.8) These minerals were formed in early geological times under high pressure.

(b) At plate boundaries where land is either being formed or destroyed. Many minerals are found along the length of the Americas, extending from the northern parts of the Rockies to the southern parts of the Andes (Figure 11.6). It is in these areas that the oceanic plates are being destroyed, creating heat as they dip under the continental plates (pages 6–8). Future exploration for minerals will take place along plate margins in the seabed, and indeed it has already begun.

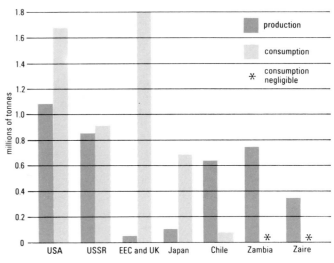

Figure 11.7 Iron ore mining in Labrador, Newfoundland

△ **Figure 11.8** Bauxite mining in Guyana

△ **Figure 11.9** (top right) World copper production and consumption

Production and refining of minerals

Here again can be seen another major difference between the developed and developing countries.

North America

(a) The USA uses over 40 per cent of the world's primary resources (including energy) yet has only 5.6 per cent of the world's population. It has large deposits of most minerals, and yet is still the major importer of 'raw' (i.e. unprocessed) minerals from the developing countries.

(b) Canada also has considerable reserves but unlike the USA, exports large amounts so that they contribute 40 per cent of her total exports in value.

Latin America

Here mineral resources are limited in comparison to North America. Latin American countries still are bound by the traditional 'colonial' economy where minerals, once mined, are exported in their 'raw state' to the developed countries. Fifty-seven per cent of South America's earnings comes from primary goods, yet this is only 25 per cent of their final prices to the consumer. These countries could earn much more if the minerals were processed before being exported. Also, several countries rely on only one mineral as their major source of income (e.g. tin in Bolivia, bauxite in Jamaica). Figure 11.9 illustrates, with reference to copper, the differences in consumption and production between developed and developing countries. To add to these difficulties many minerals are mined by multinational companies whose headquarters are in North America. This means that profits are sent overseas, and so little income is left for developing local industries, communications and services, nor does it encourage employment. Yet, if the Latin American countries became industrialised it would mean a loss of markets and a loss of raw materials (or at least an increase in their prices) for North America, and an even greater pressure put upon existing energy reserves.

Changing locations in the USA

Steel in the USA: Raw material orientated

☐ **The 1850s** The early steelworks were at Pittsburgh, Bethlehem and Phoenixville (Figure 12.1), where there were relatively local supplies of coal (the West Virginia fields), limestone and iron ore, together with rivers which could be used to transport the bulky goods. This area still produces 20 per cent of the USA's steel despite the exhaustion of the ores, its inland position and out-of-date plant.

☐ **Duluth** Grew up when the specially designed iron ore carriers taking high-grade haematite from the nearby Superior field to Pittsburgh had to return empty. As a result coal was sent in the reverse direction so that the boats were not losing money.

☐ **Great Lakes 'break-of-bulk' ports** Figure 12.2 shows how both coal and iron ore being moved between Pittsburgh and Duluth have to change their form of transport at such lakeside ports as Cleveland. With the raw materials being handled here together with a large local market, it was logical to produce steel here. Today as the Superior ores run out, more iron ore is brought from Labrador via the St Lawrence Seaway (30 per cent of the USA's total).

☐ **Coastal locations** Sparrows Point (Figure 12.3) can import the ores from Labrador and South America, is near to the east coast markets and the West Virginia coalfield, and has plenty of cheap, reclaimable land. Sparrows Point is the largest tidewater steelworks in the world, and produces 10 per cent of the USA total. Figure 12.3 shows the unloaded iron ore on the quay with the blast furnaces and then the steel strip and rolling mills behind.

Car assembly plants: raw material and market orientated

Until the 1950s, both the manufacture of car parts and the final car assembly were carried out almost entirely in the north-east of the USA, and especially around Detroit (Figure 12.4).

Locational advantages of the Detroit area

☐ Availability of such raw materials as steel.

☐ Availability of energy.

☐ Large labour force, both skilled and unskilled. The industry may become increasingly mechanised but that often means boring, repetitive work. The companies expect high productivity for their wages.

☐ Central location for the assembly of car parts, obtained from up to 2000 different firms, to keep final costs down.

☐ Large local market for car sales.

☐ The chance factor by which such people as Ford just happened to live in the area.

Present day locational factors

As the major markets for cars include both California and the East Coast 'Boswash' megalopolis, as well as the Great Lakes area, there has been a shift in the present-day location of the final vehicle assembly plants. Motor vehicles have to be assembled on continuously moving production lines, and as these are capable of completing a car every minute the plant must produce over a quarter of a million vehicles each year to be profitable. As a result, demand must be sufficiently high to absorb the cost of transporting the car parts, still mainly manufactured in the Detroit area, to the new assembly plants (see Figure 12.4).

△ **Figure 12.3** Sparrows Point

▽ **Figure 12.1** Steel in the Great Lakes area

▷ **Figure 12.2** Cleveland, a 'break-of-bulk' port

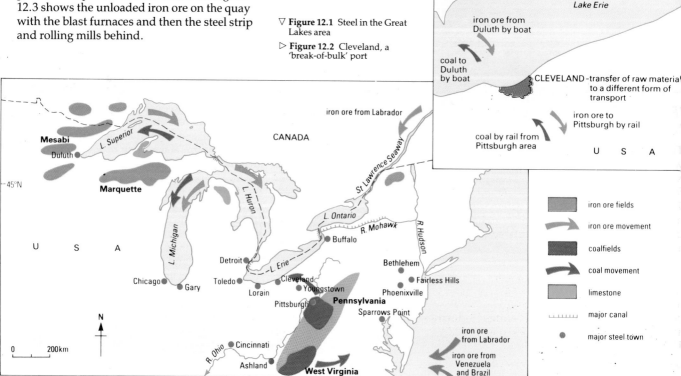

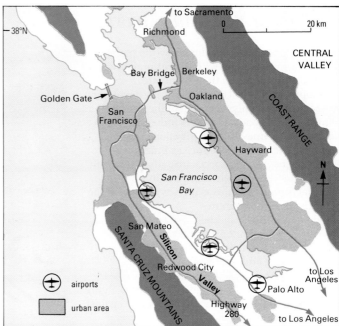

△ **Figure 12.5** Silicon Valley, California

◁ **Figure 12.4** Distribution of car assembly plants in the USA

'Footloose' industries: Market and transport orientated

The term 'footloose' is applied to those firms which have a relatively free choice of location. Many of these newer industries provide services for people and are therefore market orientated. The raw materials are often component goods made elsewhere, and the finished product is usually light and easily transportable by road or air.

The Silicon Valley (Figure 12.5), south of San Francisco Bay, has become the major centre in the USA for the new electrical and high technological industries (e.g. micro-electronics). The towns benefiting from these so-called 'sunrise' industries are strung out along Highway 280 (Figure 12.5). The advantages of the area include:

❑ The attraction of a warm, sunny climate.

❑ Ample space for development and future expansion.

❑ Distance from large cities with their high land values.

❑ Nearness to major road systems to transport the light and easily transportable raw materials and finished goods (Figure 12.5).

❑ Nearness to several airports for internal trade and export.

❑ Availability of skilled labour for high technology industries.

❑ Clean, modern sites adjacent to housing areas for labour supply.

❑ Clean and generally quiet industries which can be located near housing areas and markets.

Products made include miniaturised computers, advanced navigation and signalling equipment, and parts for the aerospace industry.

Industry in Latin America

Most countries in the developing world place industrialisation, along with agricultural progress, top of their priorities in their economic development. In 1980 the whole of the developing world produced only 9 per cent of the world's total manufactured goods. However industrialisation has been very uneven in distribution. Several Latin American countries such as Brazil and Argentina have made spectacular advances, with up to 25 per cent of their workforce in manufacturing – a figure as high as in some of the old industrialised countries.

Other countries, especially in Central America, have made very limited progress and have less than 5 per cent of their workforce in manufacturing and over 80 per cent still in agriculture. At every level industrialisation leads to drastic changes in the country's lifestyle. Figure 12.6 shows some of the arguments for and against industrialisation.

△ **Figure 12.7** Quechua woma weaving, Peru

Four suggested approaches to industrialisation

1 Agricultural industries If countries have the majority of their labour force in agriculture, industrial development should begin with the processing and refining of agricultural products (e.g. sugar refining, fruit canning).

2 Simultaneous development This is when industry and farming develop together. Industry initially depends upon local markets and so farming communities will have to increase their output to create extra money to buy the local manufactures. Higher agricultural output means less food needs to be imported and so extra money is available to invest in such 'craft' industries as basket making, clothing and leather goods (Figure 12.7), and agricultural industries such as fertilisers.

3 Export orientated industries These industries are found in countries which have had a relatively long history of national independence and where overseas investment has been made.

4 Prestige schemes These are large schemes aimed at impressing overseas countries. The hope is that further investment will result, but such schemes rarely benefit the mass of the country's population.

▷ **Figure 12.6** Should developing countries industrialise?

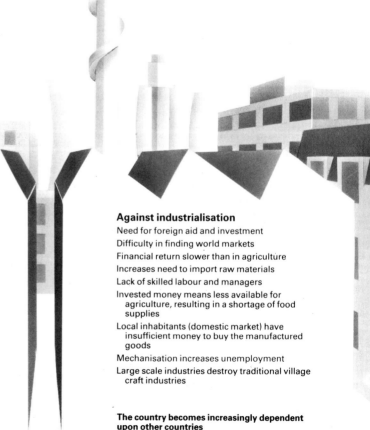

For industrialisation

Industrialisation is a status symbol-moving away from 'colonial economy'

Diversification of economy by relying less upon agriculture

Agriculture too reliant upon the unpredictable weather and world markets

Money invested in manufacturing rather than in agriculture

Reduces amount of imports

Leads to improved education, technological skills and health

Leads to development of transport and energy

Raises living standards (higher GNP)

Reduces unemployment

Produces fertilisers and farm machinery which should increase agricultural output

The country becomes increasingly economically independent of other countries

Against industrialisation

Need for foreign aid and investment

Difficulty in finding world markets

Financial return slower than in agriculture

Increases need to import raw materials

Lack of skilled labour and managers

Invested money means less available for agriculture, resulting in a shortage of food supplies

Local inhabitants (domestic market) have insufficient money to buy the manufactured goods

Mechanisation increases unemployment

Large scale industries destroy traditional village craft industries

The country becomes increasingly dependent upon other countries

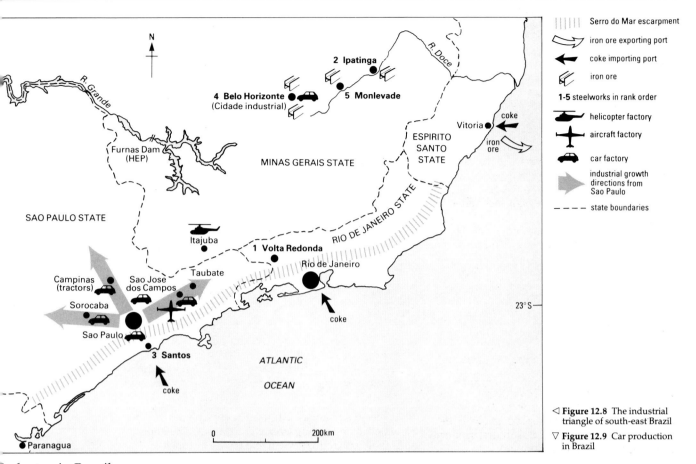

Map labels:
- R. Grande
- N
- 2 Ipatinga
- R. Doce
- 4 Belo Horizonte (Cidade industrial)
- 5 Monlevade
- Furnas Dam (HEP)
- MINAS GERAIS STATE
- ESPIRITO SANTO STATE
- Vitoria — coke
- iron ore
- SAO PAULO STATE
- Itajuba
- 1 Volta Redonda
- RIO DE JANEIRO STATE
- Rio de Janeiro
- Campinas (tractors)
- Taubate
- Sao Jose dos Campos
- Sorocaba
- Sao Paulo
- 3 Santos
- coke
- ATLANTIC OCEAN
- coke
- 23°S
- 0   200km
- Paranagua

Legend:
- |||||| Serro do Mar escarpment
- iron ore exporting port
- coke importing port
- iron ore
- **1-5** steelworks in rank order
- helicopter factory
- aircraft factory
- car factory
- industrial growth directions from Sao Paulo
- – – – – state boundaries

◁ **Figure 12.8** The industrial triangle of south-east Brazil

▽ **Figure 12.9** Car production in Brazil

Industry in Brazil

Brazil is regarded as one of the most successful of the developing countries in terms of increased industrialisation.

Steel employs 4 per cent of the total manufacturing force. There are 18 integrated and 22 semi-integrated steelworks, all in the three south-eastern states of Minas Gerais (where iron ore is mined), Sao Paulo and Rio de Janeiro (Figure 12.8). The five major steelworks are numbered, in rank order, on Figure 12.8. Brazil has to import coke from the USA, but is fortunate in being able to export iron ore in return.

The car industry Although Fords opened a factory in Sao Paulo in 1919, until the 1950s all the vehicles assembled there were exported. In 1980 Brazil produced over 1 million cars, which made it the fifth largest producer in the world. Over 3 per cent of Brazil's industrial workers help to manufacture cars. The growth has been aided by government policy which –

◻ considered that the growth of a limited number of key industries would lead to the growth of other industries,

◻ encouraged the growth of all the component part industries,

◻ granted financial aid to help the importation of specialist machinery,

◻ encouraged capital investment from multinational companies (page 92), and

◻ restricted imports to ensure complete control of the domestic market.

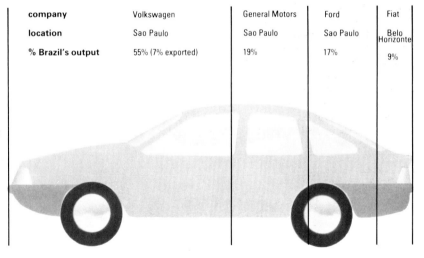

company	Volkswagen	General Motors	Ford	Fiat
location	Sao Paulo	Sao Paulo	Sao Paulo	Belo Horizonte
% Brazil's output	55% (7% exported)	19%	17%	9%

The multinational car manufacturers in Brazil are shown in Figure 12.9.

The recession of the 1980s has hit Brazil as much as the USA. In 1981 there was a drop in car sales of 40 per cent and in the first three months of that year a drop in steel demand by 25 per cent. Added to this, Brazil had an annual inflation rate of 95 per cent (in Argentina it was 130 per cent) and an annual rise in prices of 60 per cent. Unemployment is soaring in a country already short of jobs, and the foreign debt is enormous. Has Brazil's economic miracle ended?

Multinational companies

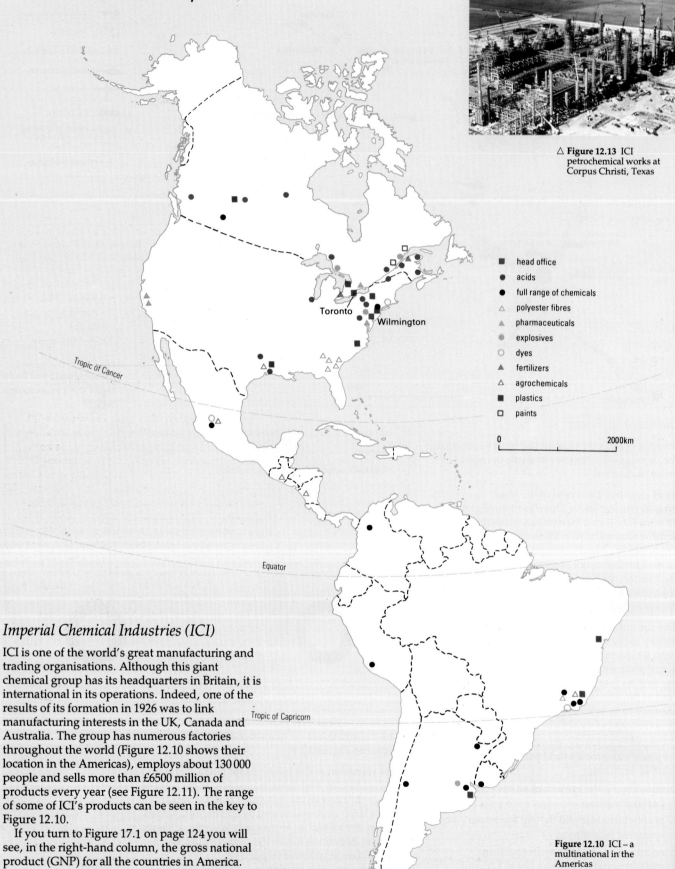

△ **Figure 12.13** ICI petrochemical works at Corpus Christi, Texas

Key:
- ■ head office
- ● acids
- ● full range of chemicals
- △ polyester fibres
- ▲ pharmaceuticals
- ● explosives
- ○ dyes
- ▲ fertilizers
- △ agrochemicals
- ■ plastics
- □ paints

Toronto

Wilmington

Tropic of Cancer

Equator

Tropic of Capricorn

0   2000km

Figure 12.10 ICI – a multinational in the Americas

Imperial Chemical Industries (ICI)

ICI is one of the world's great manufacturing and trading organisations. Although this giant chemical group has its headquarters in Britain, it is international in its operations. Indeed, one of the results of its formation in 1926 was to link manufacturing interests in the UK, Canada and Australia. The group has numerous factories throughout the world (Figure 12.10 shows their location in the Americas), employs about 130 000 people and sells more than £6500 million of products every year (see Figure 12.11). The range of some of ICI's products can be seen in the key to Figure 12.10.

If you turn to Figure 17.1 on page 124 you will see, in the right-hand column, the gross national product (GNP) for all the countries in America.

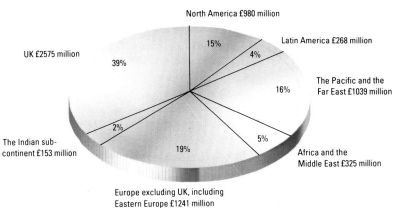

North America £980 million

Latin America £268 million

15%

4%

UK £2575 million

39%

16%

The Pacific and the Far East £1039 million

2%

5%

The Indian sub-continent £153 million

19%

Africa and the Middle East £325 million

Europe excluding UK, including Eastern Europe £1241 million

◁ **Figure 12.11** ICI – 1981 world-wide sales

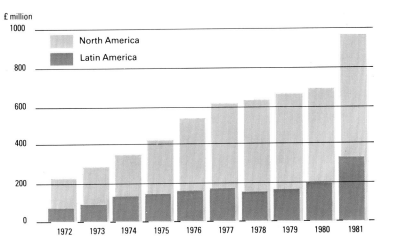

£ million

North America

Latin America

△ **Figure 12.12** ICI sales in North and Latin America

▽ **Figure 12.14** Setting up a multinational in a developing country

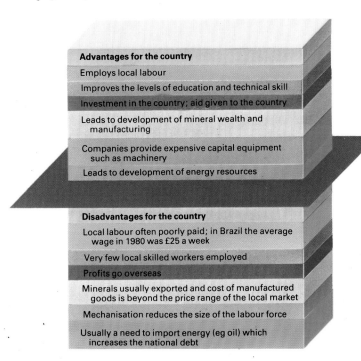

Advantages for the country

Employs local labour

Improves the levels of education and technical skill

Investment in the country; aid given to the country

Leads to development of mineral wealth and manufacturing

Companies provide expensive capital equipment such as machinery

Leads to development of energy resources

Disadvantages for the country

Local labour often poorly paid; in Brazil the average wage in 1980 was £25 a week

Very few local skilled workers employed

Profits go overseas

Minerals usually exported and cost of manufactured goods is beyond the price range of the local market

Mechanisation reduces the size of the labour force

Usually a need to import energy (eg oil) which increases the national debt

1 Rank the following countries according to their GNP: Agentina, Brazil, Bolivia, Canada, Colombia, Costa Rica, Mexico, Nicaragua, Paraguay, Peru, Uruguay and the USA.

2 Now return to Figure 12.10.

   (a) Which two countries have most ICI factories?

   (b) Which three countries have between three and eight ICI factories?

   (c) Which countries listed in question 1 above have (i) one ICI factory   (ii) None?

   (d) What correlation, if any, is there between ICI factories and GNP? Why is this?

3 Study the graphs in Figures 12.11 and 12.12. Notice the difference in sales for ICI products in North and Latin America. Is the gap a large one? Is it increasing or decreasing? Figure 12.13 shows one ICI plant in Texas. Why is it difficult for developing world countries to build factories such as these? Why do they have to rely upon such multinationals as ICI? Why do multinationals build factories in developing countries?

Decision making in a multinational company

Massey-Ferguson (UK) is part of a world-wide multinational tractor company. Because of the price depression and cost inflation of the early 1980s, the associated companies are having to concentrate production of an individual model in a specific factory or a specific country. Between 1980 and 1982, Massey-Ferguson (UK) had to sell its tractor and engine plant in Mexico to an indigenous company, reduce the size of its Brazilian factory and put its Argentinian plant into suspension because of high interest and inflation rates. In North America the Detroit tractor assembly plant was closed and its production was transferred to Canada and Europe.

Each decision was made at an international, not a national level, and was based upon commercial sense rather than sentiment or the effect which it might have upon the individual country.

The importance of a multinational in a developing country

A developing country can be said to be making progress and increasing its level of industrialisation and development by attracting multinational companies; but the question often asked is, 'But who benefits from the multinational companies' presence?' Certainly there are advantages and disadvantages. Study Figure 12.14 and see whether you can add any other advantages or disadvantages, and then try to decide yourself just how valuable multinational companies are in the developing world.

World trade

Trade takes place when countries try to balance out the uneven distribution of resources over the earth's surface. Unfortunately there is a large trade gap between the developed countries (who sell their manufactures) and the developing countries (who sell their raw materials).

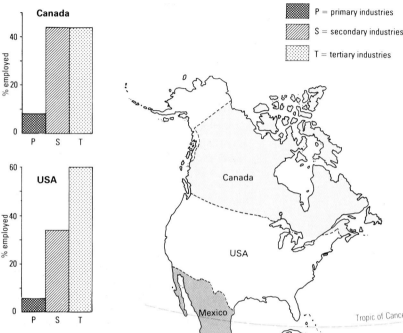

Primary products as % of exports

- ▓ over 75%
- ▒ 50-75%
- ░ 25-49%
- □ under 25%

- ▨ P = primary industries
- ▧ S = secondary industries
- ▨ T = tertiary industries

The trade of developing countries

□ Mainly primary products (foods – except cereals – minerals and timber).

□ Often only two or three items are exported.

□ Prices of these products fluctuate annually (Figure 12.16) and rise less quickly than manufactured goods.

□ Total trade of these countries is small, e.g. Latin America's exports are only a quarter of those of North America.

□ Exports are hindered by poor internal transport networks.

The trade of developed countries

□ Mainly manufactured goods and cereals.

□ Wide range of products.

□ Prices of these products have risen considerably and have little annual fluctuation.

□ Total trade of these countries is high, e.g. North America exports four times as much as Latin America.

□ Exports are helped by good internal transport networks.

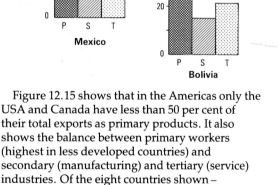

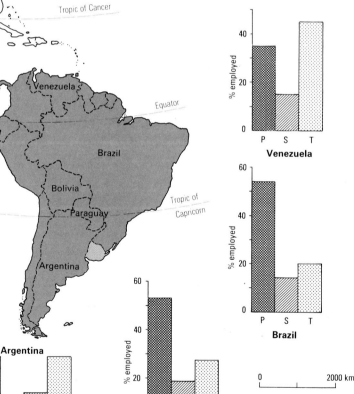

Figure 12.15 shows that in the Americas only the USA and Canada have less than 50 per cent of their total exports as primary products. It also shows the balance between primary workers (highest in less developed countries) and secondary (manufacturing) and tertiary (service) industries. Of the eight countries shown –

1 Which two have least primary workers?

2 Which two have most in secondary and tertiary industries?

3 Which five have most employed as primary workers?

4 Are these five countries, in your opinion, developing or developed countries?

5 Why does Venezuela have so many in primary and tertiary industries?

Figure 12.15 Exporters of primary products, and employment in primary, secondary and tertiary sectors

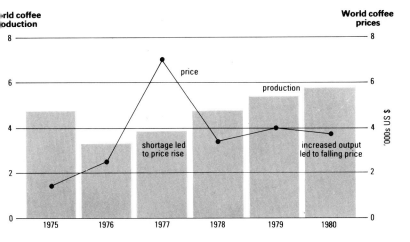

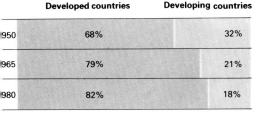

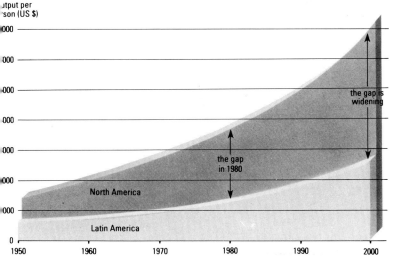

△ **Figure 12.16** Fluctuations in world coffee production and price

◁ **Figure 12.17** Percentage world trade between developed and developing countries

▽ **Figure 12.18** Trade – the widening gap

	Developed countries	Developing countries
1950	68%	32%
1965	79%	21%
1980	82%	18%

Trade between the developed and developing world is essential. The developed countries produce 90 per cent of the world's manufactures and many of these are needed by developing countries. The developing countries account for 60 per cent of the world's exports of agricultural and mineral products, which are needed by the developed countries. However, although the prices of raw materials have increased, the prices of manufactured goods have increased much more. This means that a country exporting manufactured goods earns increasingly more than a country selling raw materials – and so the trade gap widens (Figures 12.17 and 12.18). Developing countries need to try to add more value to their products before they sell them, e.g. to sell furniture rather than timber, instant coffee rather than coffee beans (this would also create more

jobs). A few middle-income countries such as Brazil, Mexico and Venezuela have become more industrialised, but for industries to grow they need to sell more in the international market. The developed countries have become worried at this extra competition and have set up trade barriers to protect their own industries.

Why are developed countries worried about industrialisation in developing countries?

They fear:

☐ Loss of markets as other countries produce their own goods.

☐ Cheaper imports from the lower-paid developing countries.

☐ Increase in unemployment as competition increases.

So barriers and tariffs are set up, and demands for total import bans are made.

But if developing countries cannot export to developed countries, they cannot earn the money needed to pay for those goods which the developed countries themselves wish to sell – with the result that world trade decreases, unemployment still grows in the developed countries, and the developing ones remain poor. According to the Brandt Report (1980 – see page 126), referring to the developed and developing worlds as the North and the South, as worries about unemployment rise in the North, the North has been putting up more barriers to manufacturers from the South. But most countries of the North sell at least four times as much to the Third World by way of manufactures (in value) than they buy from Third World Countries. And countries of the North are depending more and more on selling to the South. The more poorer countries earn by selling, the more they are able to buy from the North – thus creating more jobs in the North. As industries grow in developing countries, richer countries of the North may have to move some of their capital and workforce out of some industries and into others. While some jobs may be lost in countries like Britain because of imports from the South, at least as many new jobs are gained by increased sales to the South. A 1980 ILO report shows that if the North were to import 11% more manufactures a year from the South (instead of the expected 8.8%) the North would still be gaining a net 28,000 jobs a year from North–South trade. *'This structured change in the world economy is inevitable and will bring many mutual gains in the long run. It is therefore alarming that the North has shown signs of turning away from adjustment towards intensified protection.'* As the Brandt Report also says, *'a significant proportion of jobs in the North depend on trade with the South. There will be difficult conflicts within the North between those who have to change their employment and those who do not. But if the North fails to adjust, it will be more difficult for everybody.'*

Changes in Brazil

Figure 13.1 shows the major roads in Brazil in 1982. The greatest concentration is in the more industrialised and urbanised south-east of the country. Many of these roads linked coastal ports but few extended very far inland.

Trans-Amazonica Highway (Figure 13.2)

1 Why, until the 1970s, were so few roads built in the tropical rainforests?

2 How long is the Trans-Amazonica Highway between Recife and Rio Branco?

3 Why was this highway not built next to the Amazon?

4 How and why are roads in the tropical rainforest built differently to those in the south-east of the country?

5 What do you consider to be the major problems in building highways in the tropical rainforest?

Why was the Trans-Amazonica Highway built?

☐ To link the Brazilian coast with the interior and the Peruvian border.

☐ To attract 'colonists' and new settlements to try to reduce population pressures in the coastal areas (page 38) and the drought-stricken Sertao (pages 66–7).

☐ To develop new farming lands, especially for ranching (page 53), and to exploit timber resources.

☐ To help explore and then exploit valuable mineral resources.

The effect that this and other Amazonian highways have had on the environment and the Amerindians is described on page 120.

Modern motorways in south-east Brazil

As both population and industry continue to grow and the country improves its wealth, and as new road building techniques are developed, modern highways such as that shown in Figure 13.3 can be constructed.

Figure 13.1 Brazil's road network, 1982

Legend:
— paved highway
– – – under construction
········· gravel road

△ **Figure 13.3** Modern road near Rio de Janeiro

▷ **Figure 13.2** Trans-Amazonica Highway

Traditional forms in Latin America

Large tracts of Latin America still lack any form of modern transport. This is partly because of the shortage of money which is needed to bring communications up to the standard of North America, and partly because much of Latin America poses severe physical constraints upon the building of roads, railways and airports.

The Incas, living high up in the Andes, have been the only major civilisation in history to have developed without the use of the wheel; not because they were unaware of its existence but because of its limitations on the steep mountain sides. Instead the Incas (as do their descendants) used the donkey (Figure 13.4) and the llama (Figure 13.5) as beasts of burden.

Within much of tropical America large rivers have afforded the only easy routes into the interior. Even today many American tribes still use the dugout canoe as their major form of moving about in the forest. Figure 13.6 shows the Lacandon tribe (see also page 53) who live in Belize and western Guatemala.

Even more traditional are the Totora reed boats which are used by the Oru tribe who fish in lake Titicaca (Figure 13.7). These reeds also provide the 'ground' for this tribe to live on for, as the bottom layers rot, the Indians spread new layers on top to form floating islands.

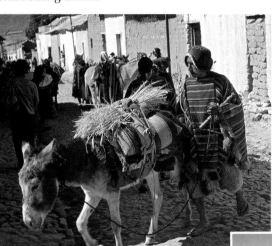

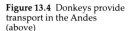

Figure 13.4 Donkeys provide transport in the Andes (above)

Figure 13.5 Traditional forms of transport in the Andes (right)

Figure 13.6 Dugout canoes are still used by Lacandon Indians in Central America (top right)

Figure 13.7 Reeds provide the material for building boats and houses beside Lake Titicaca (far right)

Transcontinental highways

The 1970s saw the building of several major transcontinental highways in the more isolated parts of Latin America, and the extension northwards of the already existing North American network (Figure 13.8).

□ Many Latin American countries, along with other developing countries in the world, had very poor communications. The hope was that by building highways, countries could export more food products, which normally would have perished before reaching large urban markets, and also minerals. The USA gave aid to several countries which joined together to build the Trans-American Highway, but it was the USA which benefited most from the resultant increase in trade.

□ Other highways have been constructed in order to open up new areas, such as the tropical rainforests for farming and minerals, and the Alaskan Highway for minerals in the Arctic.

□ Highways have also been built for political and strategic reasons – partly as prestige symbols and partly to control distant and often disputed territorial frontiers.

In Latin America many of these so-called highways are indeed only single carriageway and are only metalled in parts (Figure 13.2). Their initial construction and the subsequent maintenance costs are enormous. Indeed a question facing many poorer countries is, 'Can we develop without good roads, and yet can we afford the cost of new highways?'

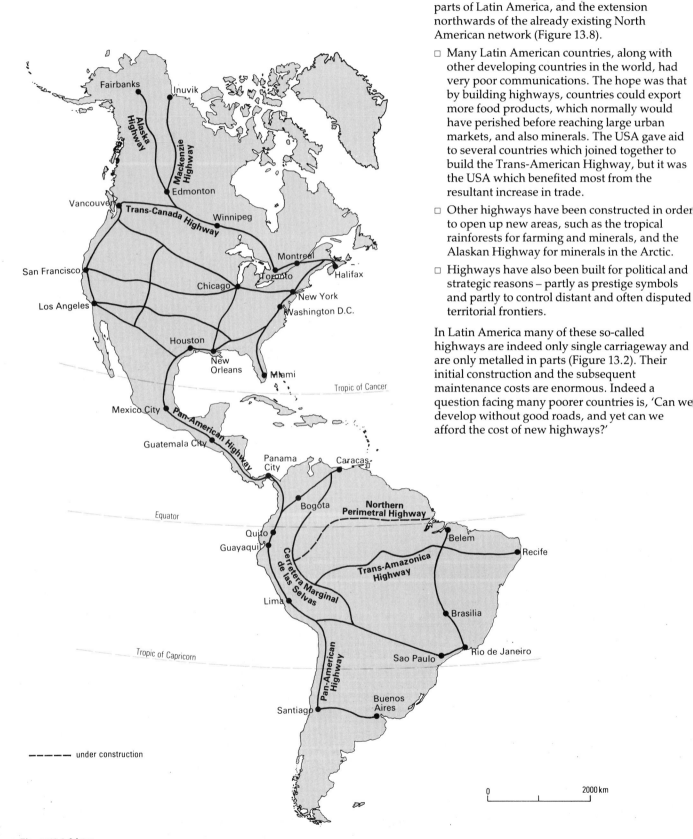

Figure 13.8 Major transcontinental roads in the Americas

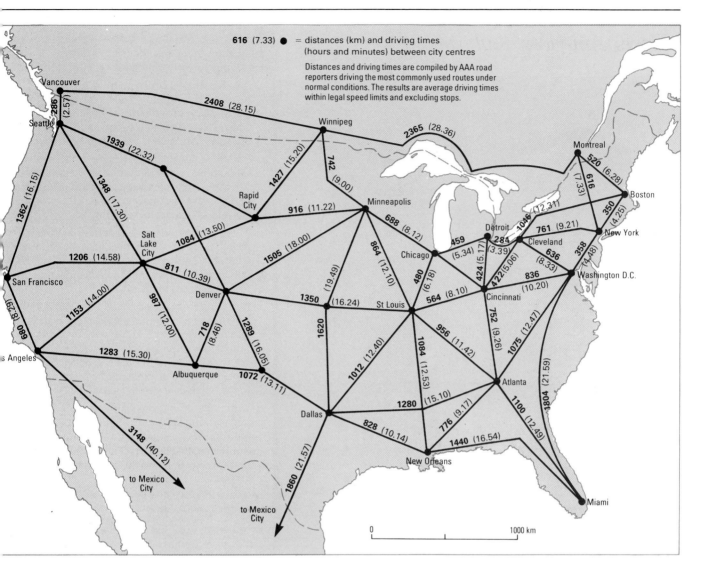

616 (7.33) ● = distances (km) and driving times (hours and minutes) between city centres

Distances and driving times are compiled by AAA road reporters driving the most commonly used routes under normal conditions. The results are average driving times within legal speed limits and excluding stops.

Vancouver 286 (2.57)
Seattle 2408 (28.15) Winnipeg
1939 (22.32) 2365 (28.36) Montreal 520 (6.28)
1362 (16.15) 1348 (17.30) 616 (7.33) Boston
1427 (15.20) 742 (9.00) 350 (4.25)
Rapid City 1046 (12.31) New York
1084 (13.50) 916 (11.22) Minneapolis Detroit 761 (9.21)
Salt Lake City 1505 (18.00) 688 (8.12) 459 (5.34) 284 (3.39) Cleveland 358 (4.48)
1206 (14.58) 811 (10.39) 864 (12.10) Chicago 424 (5.17) 221 (5.06) 636 (8.33) Washington D.C.
San Francisco 1153 (14.00) 987 (12.00) Denver 1350 (16.24) 480 (8.9) 564 (8.10) 836 (10.20) Cincinnati
898 (8.29) 718 (8.46) 1289 (16.05) 1620 St Louis 956 (11.42) 752 (9.26) 1075 (12.47)
s Angeles 1283 (15.30) Albuquerque 1072 (13.11) 1012 (12.40) 1084 (12.53) 1804 (21.59) Atlanta
690 (8.28) 1280 (15.10) 776 (9.17) 1100 (12.49)
3148 (40.12) Dallas 828 (10.14) 1440 (16.54)
to Mexico City 1860 (21.57) New Orleans Miami
to Mexico City
0   1000 km

The Interstate and the Superhighway system of the USA and southern Canada

In the USA financial assistance has long been given for road construction. The federal purposes of interstate highways include:

- [ ] Connecting the major metropolitan centres and industrial areas by limited access, high-speed roads, with appropriate cross-border links with Canada and Mexico.

- [ ] Improving the nation's defence potential in the event of war.

- [ ] Improving the national economy by speeding up the flow of goods and people across the country. This has led to the decentralisation of industry from the north-east of the country, e.g. cars (page 89) and aeroplanes to California.

These interstate highways are essential to a nation of car owners, and have led to the growth of the trucking industry. Study the map (Figure 13.9).

1 What is the shortest (a) time (b) distance between the Pacific and the Atlantic coasts of the USA? Through which cities does this route pass?

2 What are the advantages and disadvantages of a map drawn in this way?

Lengthy journeys between American cities have seen the growth of many overnight 'route centres' and the development of luxury coaches (Figure 13.10).

△ **Figure 13.9** Average driving times and distances in the USA (top)

△ **Figure 13.10** Transcontinental coaches in New York

North American Railways

AMTRAK In 1971 the US Federal Government created this official corporation to pay railway companies to retain and improve the few surviving inter-city and cross-country routes.

☐ All-electric (190 km/h) metroliners operate between Washington, New York and Boston. These can get from central Washington to central New York in less time (and more cheaply) than by air, and in half the time taken by a car.

☐ Operations are concentrated along important 'corridor' routes between large urban areas e.g. San Diego–Los Angeles; Dallas–Houston; and Cleveland–Chicago.

☐ There is a limited number of transcontinental trains (three per day between New York and Chicago). Figure 1.4 shows how long it takes between New York and Los Angeles compared to the six hours by plane.

☐ Resulting from the oil crisis of the 1970s, came an American awareness of the need to develop their own resources, and especially the easily mined low sulphur coals west of the Mississippi (page 78). Although some is sent by coal slurry pipeline, much is transferred by new rail track to the north-east states (Figure 13.12).

☐ Unit trains, consisting of identical rolling stock and running between specific points with an identical load, are economic because they have low labour costs and high utilisation ratios. The main commodities carried are grain, iron ore and coal.

☐ 'Containerisation' has brought together road and rail transport.

By the 1980s rail employment was beginning to rise as more freight and passengers were carried, new tracks were laid and the continual rise in oil prices made the railways more competitive.

During the 1960s, the increase in road and air traffic was accompanied by a sharp decline in the number of passengers and amount of freight carried by rail. In the USA in particular, railway companies were going bankrupt, stations were being demolished, freight yards were sold for urban development and thousands of kilometres of track were closed. By 1970 only 1 per cent of inter-city travellers went by train. North of the border in Canada, the two companies of the CPR (Canadian Pacific Railway) and CNR (Canadian National Railway) competed for a declining market.

VIA This was created in 1978 in Canada by the amalgamation of the CPR and the CNR. New, faster trains (Figure 13.11) operate both local and transcontinental routes.

△ **Figure 13.11** VIA passenger train

▷ **Figure 13.12** Freight train carrying coal in Virginia. These trains may be pulled by as many as five engines and consist of up to 100 freight cars

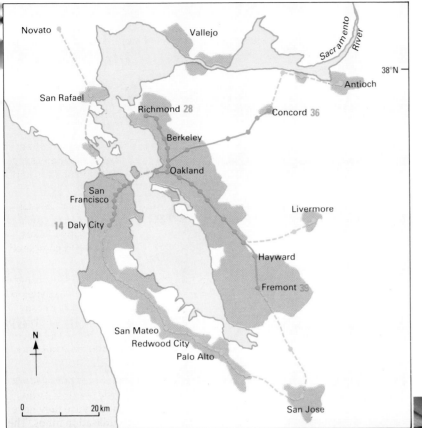

Routes: 1 Daly City - Richmond
        2 Daly City - Concord
        3 Daly City - Fremont
        4 Fremont - Richmond

urban areas

BART routes and stations

possible BART extensions

BART tunnel

39 peak hour travel time to CBD

◁ **Figure 13.13** Bay Area Rapid Transit system

BART – the San Francisco Bay Area Rapid Transit System.

Like many other large cities, San Francisco receives thousands of commuters each weekday. During the 1960s an increasingly larger percentage travelled by car, causing pollution (noise, fumes and visual), accidents and congestion, and making demands upon the city authorities to construct more freeways and car parks. Originally planned in 1957, opened in 1974 and completed in 1978, the Bay Area Rapid Transit system (Figure 13.13) is a 120 km underwater, underground, and elevated electric railway designed to ease traffic congestion in the CBD. At the centre is a double-barrelled prefabricated tube (flexible to withstand earthquakes) which passes underneath San Francisco Bay.

△ **Figure 13.14** High speed electric BART train

Advantages

- Electric and so pollution free (Figure 13.14).
- Fast conveyance of 200 000 commuters a day in 1980 (double by 1990?)
- Trains can travel up to 120 km/h. The time over the bay between Oakland and San Francisco is 9 minutes (11 km) instead of over 40 minutes at peak times by road.
- Trains run every 1½ minutes at peak times, and 20 minutes through the night.
- Modern carriages are noiseless, air conditioned and carpeted.
- The whole system is 'fully automatic and computerised' – drivers only take over in an emergency.
- Long platforms ensure rapid alighting and boarding.
- Lower fares than by bus to attract users.
- Cars left at suburban stations reduce CBD congestion.
- Regeneration of commercial life in the CBD.

Disadvantages

- Twin problems of traffic congestion and car parking have been shifted to suburban stations.
- Lack of car parking space and buses at suburban stations.
- Limited reliability because of technical problems.
- System operates at a loss estimated to be over £2 per passenger carried.

101

Commuting

As urban areas have grown, inner city areas have become less desirable for living in and, as mobility has increased, more people (especially the better off) have moved their homes further and further from their place of work. These commuters live in towns and villages and face long and often expensive journeys to their work, which may well be in the city centre. Figure 13.15 shows how far people are prepared to travel to work in Chicago. (The maximum distance is the boundary of Chicago's commuter hinterland.) How far are people prepared to travel into central Chicago?

There is one anomaly in commuter patterns in many North American cities – the black Americans. This group tends to live in low cost housing near the city centre, whereas many of today's less skilled jobs, still filled by a large proportion of the black population, are now found on estates on the edge of cities. So this group of 'commuters' have to travel outwards from the central areas.

Problems caused by commuters in city centres

- ☐ Congestion, especially at peak hours, because most commuters prefer to travel by car.
- ☐ Air pollution from car exhausts – a problem especially acute in Los Angeles (smog).
- ☐ Noise pollution from cars and lorries.
- ☐ Parking problems.
- ☐ Increased risk of accidents.
- ☐ Cost of building urban freeways (Figure 13.16), many of which are multi-lane.
- ☐ Destruction of existing houses and open space to create urban freeways (see plan of Los Angeles in Figure 13.17).
- ☐ Reduction in land values of property adjacent to urban freeways.

- ☐ Often, in America, a decline in public transport meant increased hardship to the minority non-car owners. Only recently have cities such as Seattle, Atlanta, Washington DC, and San Francisco tried to introduce new rapid transit public transport systems (page 101).

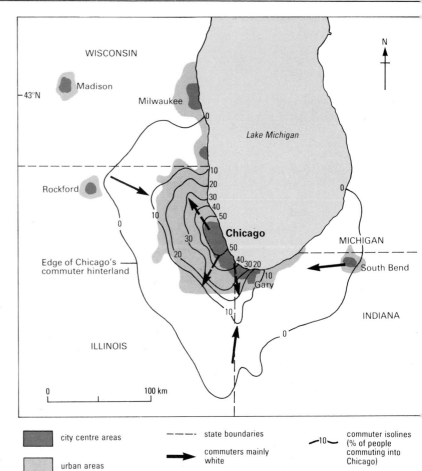

■ city centre areas	
▨ urban areas	

- - - - - state boundaries
➡ commuters mainly white
⇢ mainly black
⌒10⌒ commuter isolines (% of people commuting into Chicago)

△ **Figure 13.15** Commuting in Chicago

▽ **Figure 13.16 and 13.17** Urban freeways, Los Angeles

Shopping patterns

The CBD

The central nucleus of shops used to be in the city centre where converging routes gave the greatest accessibility. Since 1960 there has been a tendency for more shops to move away from the city centre to areas where their customers live and land is cheaper (Figure 13.18). In response many city centres have totally remodernised themselves with traffic-free precincts (Figure 13.19) and large department stores and specialist shops selling high-order durable goods.

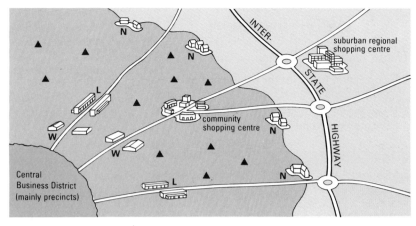

L linear/ribbon centres

N local neighbourhood shopping centre

W wholesale areas

▲ residential area of city with corner shops

△ **Figure 13.18** Model showing shopping centres within a North American city

◁ **Figure 13.19** Minneapolis shopping centre

▽ **Figure 13.20** Stonestown shopping centre, San Francisco

Central ring of varying patterns

Note the following features:

☐ Ribbon development of shops, especially wholesalers, along main roads leading into the CBD.

☐ Community shopping centres with a small nucleus of shops at major road junctions.

☐ Small neighbourhood shopping centres selling non-durable goods for local housing estates.

☐ Small, isolated corner shops selling low-order, convenience goods.

Modern suburban shopping centres
(Figure 13.20).

These have drastically affected the turnover of other shops because most cities in North America now have large, planned regional shopping centres on their periphery. Here over 200 stores may be covered by one huge roof, and the whole complex is surrounded by car parks capable of taking several thousand vehicles. Access from major roads (Figure 13.20) is essential. Such centres, built upon cheap land, often farmland, usually include cinemas, theatres, restaurants, skating rinks and play areas, so that they are geared to the whole family. Such 'superstores' will sell every commodity in bulk at reduced prices.

Water transport

The St Lawrence Seaway

1 Using Figure 13.21, list the natural obstacles to navigation in the Great Lakes–St Lawrence area.

2 Using Figure 13.22, say which of these problems have been overcome, and which still remain.

The building of the St Lawrence Seaway

Canals linking the Great Lakes, and bypassing parts of the St Lawrence rapids, had been built in stages since 1855. However, it was still impossible for ocean-going vessels to reach the ports of the Great Lakes. In 1954, after numerous attempts at persuasion by the Canadians, the US Government finally agreed to help build a seaway. This was officially opened in 1959.

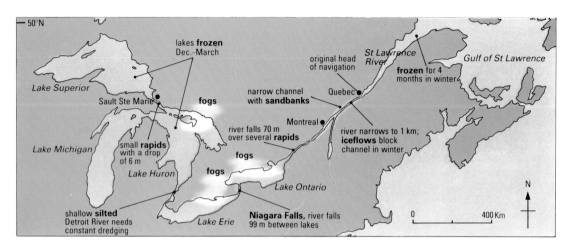

◁ **Figure 13.21** Obstacles to navigation in the Great Lakes – St Lawrence area

▽ **Figure 13.22** How some problems to navigation have been overcome

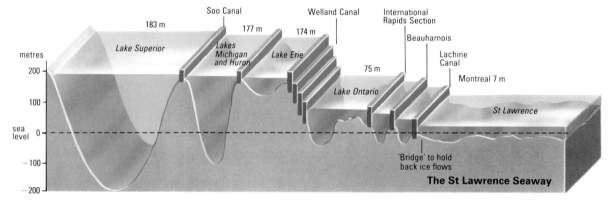

◁ **Figure 13.23** St Lambert Locks on the St Lawrence Seaway

Advantages of the Seaway

- Ocean-going vessels of up to 25 000 tons can now sail 3700 km up to the ports of Chicago and Thunder Bay without having to break their journey. The minimum depth of 8 metres also admits vessels of deeper draught (Figure 13.23).
- Hydro-electric power stations were also built (page 80).
- The interior industrial areas of the Great Lakes and the agricultural regions of the Great Plains and Mid-West have increased their trading outlets.

Trade on the St Lawrence Seaway

Using your knowledge and Figures 6.18, 9.10 and 12.1, list the major cargoes carried (a) eastwards (b) westwards.

The Panama Canal

The Panama Canal was built to shorten the journey between the east and west coasts of North America. The only two alternative sea routes were:

(a) Around the north of Canada; but this is frozen in winter.

(b) Around the south of America (Cape Horn); but this is a long way and stormy.

The Panama Canal was cut (Figure 13.24):

(a) Where the neck (isthmus) of land joining the Americas is at its narrowest.

(b) Where the mountain range (Rockies–Andes) is at its lowest.

The Canal is 80 km long and 13 m deep. Before it was constructed large areas of malarial swamps were drained. The Canal was opened in 1914 (Figure 13.25).

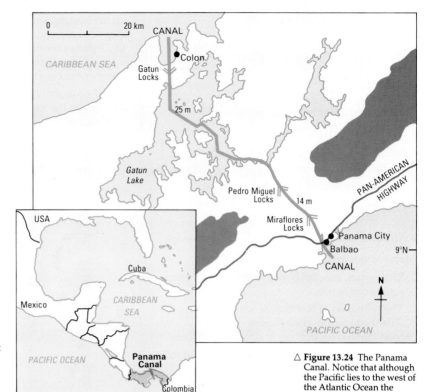

△ **Figure 13.24** The Panama Canal. Notice that although the Pacific lies to the west of the Atlantic Ocean the Pacific entrance to the Canal lies to the east of the Caribbean entrance

The importance of the Panama Canal

The Canal is important because:

- It reduces the sea journey from New York to Los Angeles by 12 000 km.
- It is of strategic value because it allows the US fleet to pass between the Atlantic and Pacific Oceans.
- It provides a quicker route from Great Britain and Western Europe to Australia and New Zealand.

◁ **Figure 13.25** Shipping on the Panama Canal

Coastal ports

As Figure 13.26 shows, there is a considerable difference between the size of ports and cargo handled by the North American ports compared with those in Latin America.

Name from your background knowledge:

1 The two large Canadian ports.

2 (a) The two largest ports on the west coast of the USA.

(b) The five largest ports on the east coast.

(c) The three largest ports on the Gulf of Mexico.

3 The four relatively large ports in Latin America.

Major routes and their cargoes include:

□ The eastern coast of North America: machinery, coal and iron ore.

□ The east coast of North America across the Atlantic to North-West Europe: mainly foodstuffs, coal, iron ore and timber products.

□ The west coast of North America: food sent to Eastern Asia, and Japanese goods returned.

□ The Panama Canal: linking the east and west coasts of the USA.

□ Latin America to North America: mainly minerals and foodstuffs.

□ Latin America to North-West Europe: raw materials sent to Europe, manufactured goods imported.

Ocean transport is still the cheapest method of moving bulky, non-perishable goods, but recently

□ Ships have become increasingly specialised and are built to carry just one type of commodity, e.g. iron-ore tankers, grain ships.

□ Ships have become larger, which has meant that wider, deeper and more sheltered estuaries are needed.

□ The so-called container revolution has speeded up the loading and unloading of cargo. Some ships can carry over 2000 containers. Figure 13.27 shows containers on the quayside at the ice-free Canadian port of Halifax awaiting shipment to North-West Europe.

□ A decline in world trade has led to both a decrease in the number of ships and ports needed and an increase in port unemployment.

□ The number of passenger cruise liners has increased, especially in the Caribbean Sea (page 117).

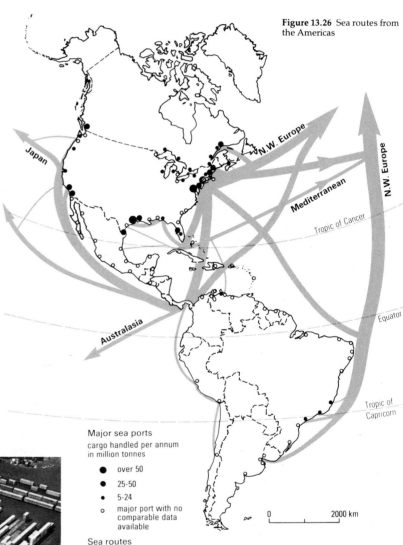

Figure 13.26 Sea routes from the Americas

Major sea ports
cargo handled per annum in million tonnes

● over 50

● 25-50

• 5-24

○ major port with no comparable data available

Sea routes

➡ principal sea lane

0   2000 km

◁ **Figure 13.27** Containers on the quayside at Halifax

Air communications

Figure 1.1 showed the size of the Americas. As a means of moving goods and people quickly, air travel has reduced travelling time enormously compared with all other forms of transport (Figure 13.28).

▷ **Figure 13.28** Reduction in travel times between Los Angeles and New York

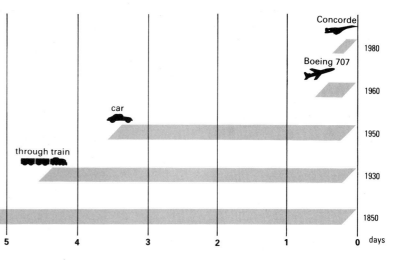

Concorde

1980

Boeing 707

1960

car

1950

through train

1930

stage coach

1850

21 days

5   4   3   2   1   0   days

Speed is essential for businessmen, holidaymakers, and the movement of lightweight perishable goods as well as emergency supplies. Air travel is needed to link isolated communities, such as the Inuits of North Canada, a West Indian island, or a mining settlement on the Canadian Shield or in the Andean States, with the outside world.

Problems of air transport

- □ Expensive use of land for constructing long runways and large terminal buildings.
- □ Expensive use of fuel to fly the planes.
- □ Adverse effect upon the environment (noise, fumes), leading to conflict with conservationists.
- □ Poorer countries 'borrow' to build prestige airports rather than improving local housing and roads.

Specialised air transport

- □ Helicopters (Figure 13.29) which can land on difficult terrain, e.g. on ice, in deserts, on mountains and in tropical forests, and can reach isolated areas which lack permanent runways.
- □ Seaplanes which can land on water in such difficult environments as the lakes of the Canadian Shield or the rivers in the tropical rainforest (Figure 13.30).
- □ Strategic planes, allegedly built for defensive purposes.

◁ **Figure 13.29** Helicopter, suitable for Arctic conditions, over the tundra in Canada

△ **Figure 13.30** Plane specially designed for landing on water

RECREATION AND TOURISM
Banff National Park

Canada's National Park system began in 1885 with the reservation of land around the mineral hot springs at Banff. Today, as the advertisement in Figure 14.1 shows, it is a major tourist area. Using Figure 14.2, list the major natural attractions of the park.

Banff Springs

Banff Springs lies 362 km west of Edmonton and 130 km north-west of Calgary. Access to the town is by 'Via' railway or the Trans-Canada Highway. It is located in the valley of the Bow river and is surrounded by high mountains (Figure 14.6). It is possible to see elk, deer and black bears wandering about the streets.

The resort originally grew up around the health-restoring warm springs. In the warm summer days it is an ideal spot for climbing, riding and walking along woodland trails (or just taking scenic chairlifts to vantage points); for cruising, boating and fishing on lake Minnewanka; or going on raft tours on the Bow river. In winter the snow-covered mounains are ideal for skiing and the lakes for skating. Throughout the year tours operate to such places in Banff National Park as Lake Louise and the Columbia icefields (Figures 14.3, 14.4, 14.5).

◁ **Figure 14.2** Attractions of Banff National Park

△ **Figure 14.3** Lake Louise

△ **Figure 14.4** Columbia Icefield

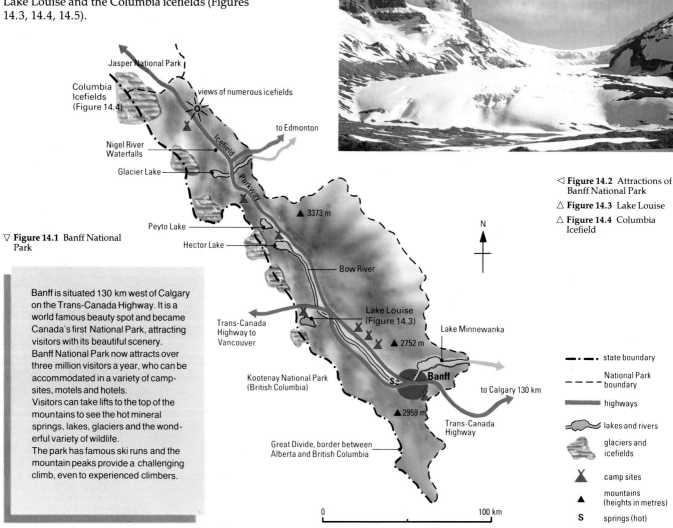

▽ **Figure 14.1** Banff National Park

Banff is situated 130 km west of Calgary on the Trans-Canada Highway. It is a world famous beauty spot and became Canada's first National Park, attracting visitors with its beautiful scenery.
Banff National Park now attracts over three million visitors a year, who can be accommodated in a variety of camp-sites, motels and hotels.
Visitors can take lifts to the top of the mountains to see the hot mineral springs, lakes, glaciers and the wonderful variety of wildlife.
The park has famous ski runs and the mountain peaks provide a challenging climb, even to experienced climbers.

Accommodation in Banff ranges from well-equipped campsites to motels and the world-famous Banff Springs Hotel (Figure 14.6 and 14.7). Other attractions in Banff include the arts festival, lasting from May to August, and wildlife and cultural museums. The peak tourist season is July and August, with a secondary peak in mid-winter. The least busy times are in spring, autumn and during midweeks.

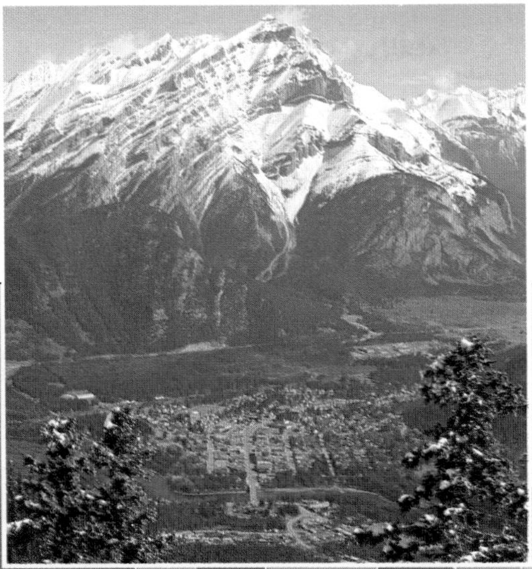

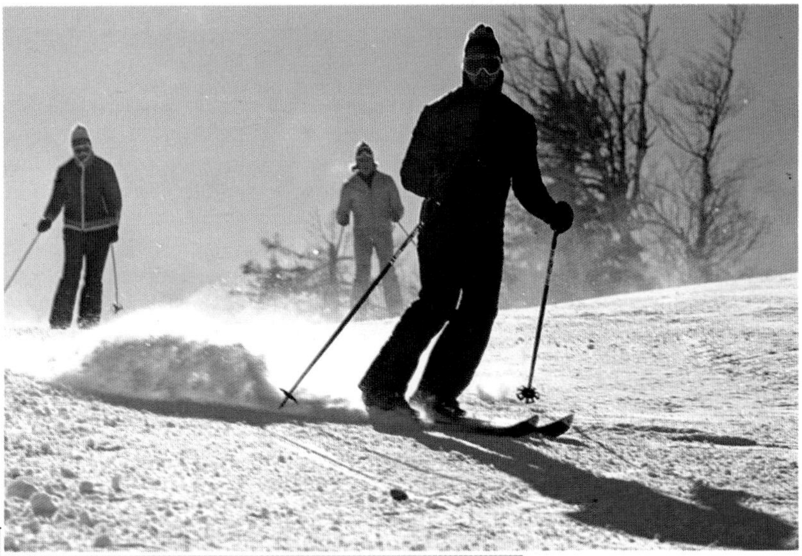

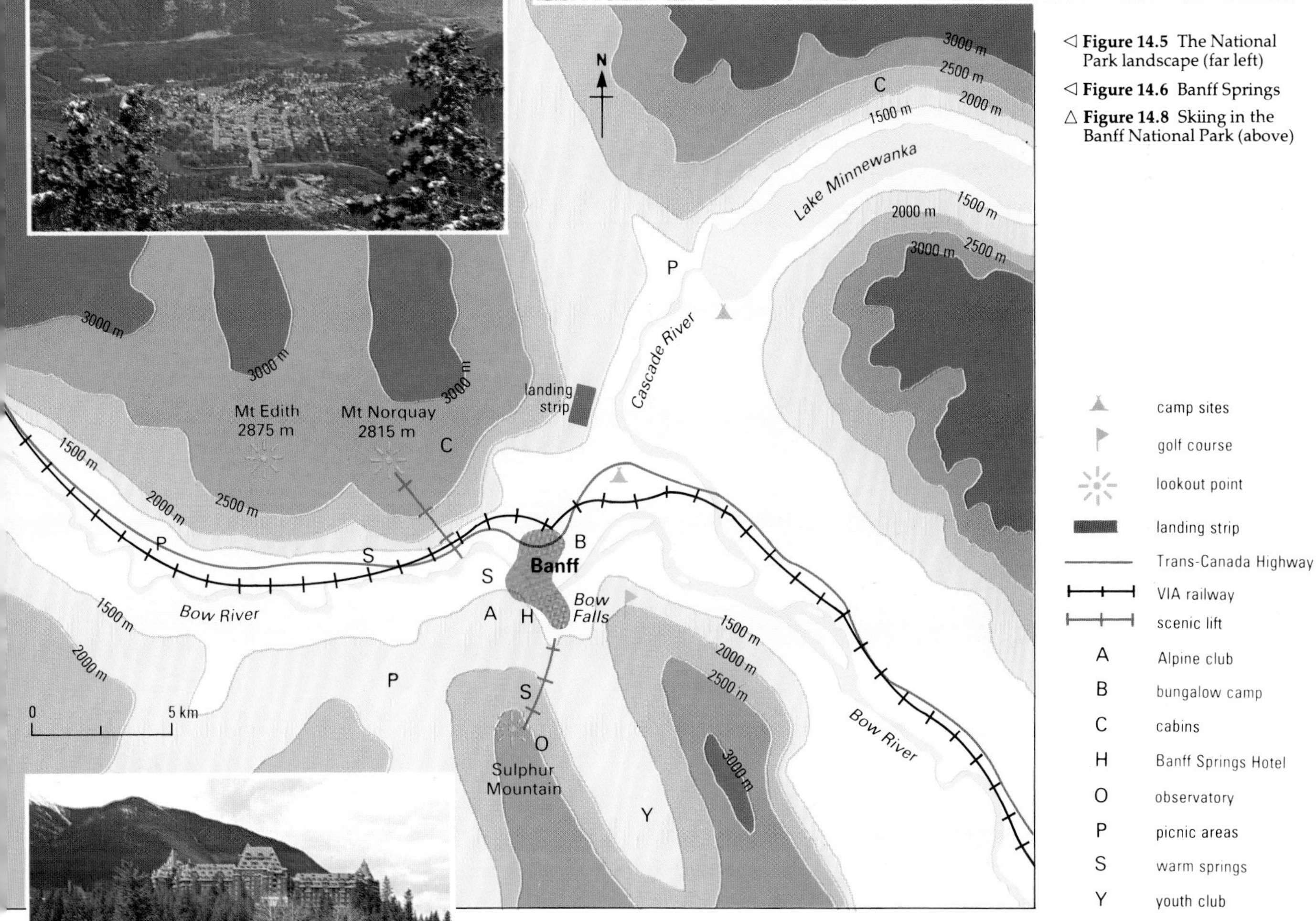
N
3000 m
2500 m
2000 m
1500 m
C
Lake Minnewanka
P
Cascade River
landing strip
Mt Edith
2875 m
Mt Norquay
2815 m
C
B
Banff
S
S
A
H
Bow Falls
Bow River
P
S
O
Sulphur Mountain
Y
Bow River
0
5 km
camp sites
golf course
lookout point
landing strip
Trans-Canada Highway
VIA railway
scenic lift
A Alpine club
B bungalow camp
C cabins
H Banff Springs Hotel
O observatory
P picnic areas
S warm springs
Y youth club

◁ **Figure 14.5** The National Park landscape (far left)

◁ **Figure 14.6** Banff Springs

△ **Figure 14.8** Skiing in the Banff National Park (above)

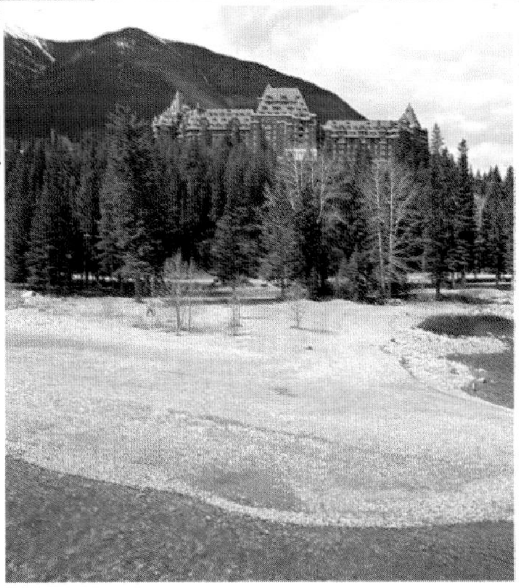

◁ **Figure 14.7** Banff Springs Hotel

Using all the information on these two pages, answer the following questions:

1 What are the natural attractions of Banff Springs?

2 What are the most important man-made attractions?

3 How can tourists reach Banff?

4 What forms of accommodation are available to tourists?

5 Describe and give reasons for the pattern of tourist visits throughout the year.

National Parks

Following the creation of the Yosemite State Park in 1864 came the world's first national park at Yellowstone in 1872 (Figure 14.9). By 1983 there were 38 national parks in the USA, 28 in Canada and others in most countries of Latin America.

National parks are created by Acts of Government to protect areas of outstanding scenery and wildlife so that they can be appreciated by urban dwellers.

Aims of North American National Parks

□ To protect areas of wilderness which were still in their natural state (unlike Western Europe where much land had already been farmed or put to other use). Usually over 90 per cent of an American National Park is wilderness (e.g. desert, mountain, caverns, tundra).

□ More often than not to protect wildlife as much as the scenery (e.g. bison, bears).

□ To encourage city dwellers to have a change of environment.

□ To cover large areas of wilderness.

□ To limit access of certain routes.

□ To limit overnight accommodation and over use.

The location of North American parks is shown in Figure 14.9. What do you notice about their location and (a) the physical landscape (Chapter 1) and (b) the distribution of population (Figure 4.14)?

Figure 14.10 shows the various types of land ownership in the USA of the national parks, the national sites and monuments, the national forest parks and other recreational areas.

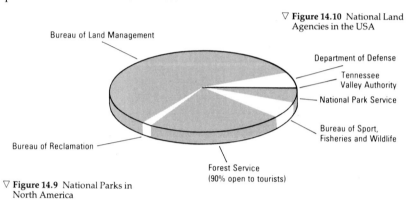

▽ **Figure 14.10** National Land Agencies in the USA

▽ **Figure 14.9** National Parks in North America

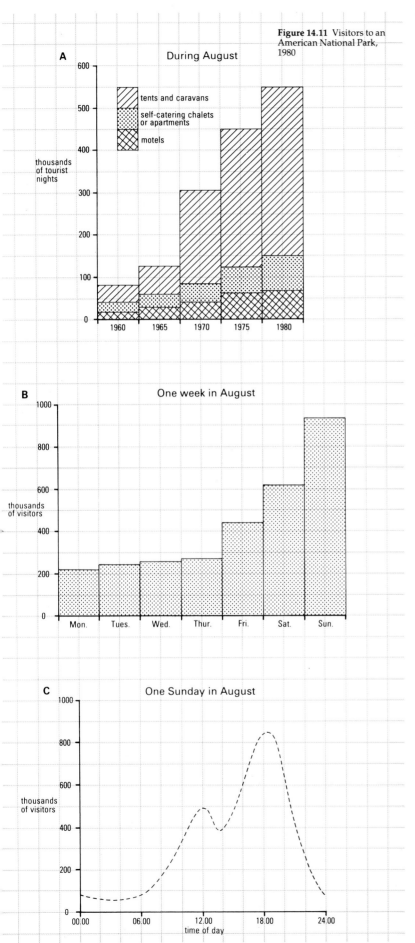

Figure 14.11 Visitors to an American National Park, 1980

Pressure on the land

- **Overcrowding at certain times of the year**, e.g. bank holidays, in summer, at weekends (Figure 14.11B) and in afternoons (Figure 14.11C).
- **Overcrowding of certain routes**, especially the access roads to the parks and the major scenic routes within the parks.
- **Over-use of amenities**, as more people visit the parks (Figure 14.11A) and the environment is spoilt (e.g. footpaths, flowers and vegetation), and people have longer waits to use man-made amenities (e.g. cafés).
- **Problems of creating car parks**
- **Problems of providing overnight accommodation** The national parks try to limit hotels and permanent buildings and to encourage campers and caravanners (Figure 14.11A). However, by midday in summer all the campsites and caravan parks are usually full.
- **Problems of pollution** caused by litter, noise and vandalism.
- **Overcrowding near car parks**, because 90 per cent of tourists do not go more than half a kilometre from their cars.
- **New forms of transport**, such as motorcycles and snowmobiles, which give access to wider, more remote areas.
- **Conflict between different users of the land** This can include conflicts between tourists and local inhabitants (scenic value against local jobs) and between different 'types' of visitor, e.g. those interested in active pursuits (water-skiing, horse riding) and those interested in passive activities (bird watching).
- **Second homes** In North America the joint appeal of increased recreational opportunities and the chance to own a piece of rural land has led to a boom in second homes. Whereas in 1970 some 40 000 second homes were built, on plots of land averaging two hectares, by 1980 this figure had risen to 100 000 a year. Buyers, who have probably never seen their land before its purchase, pay artificially high prices. The greatest pressure on land in this respect is in the east, near the urban-industrialised parts of the country.

Increased need for planning

- Control of cars. Cars are now banned in the Yosemite National Park following week-end summer peaks of 1 million per day. A shuttle bus service now operates.
- Restricting access to certain controlled routes, e.g. Great Smokey (within two days' drive for half of North America's population), Sequoia and King's Canyon National Parks.
- Controlled construction of roads, motels, camps and recreational amenities.
- Providing all-year-round amenities to spread out the time of visits.
- Catering for all users and inhabitants of the park.

Florida – the Sunshine State

Miami – a luxury resort

Miami (located on Figure 14.12) is a major resort for the following reasons.

Natural advantages

☐ High summer temperatures and long hours of sunshine (Figure 14.13), yet not too humid because of sea-breezes.

☐ Warm winters (January 16°C) because of its sub-tropical location and the offshore Gulf Stream current.

☐ Warm, clear, blue seas.

☐ Natural sandbars giving 24 km of sandy beaches.

☐ A lagoon which gives shelter for yachts against the autumn hurricanes.

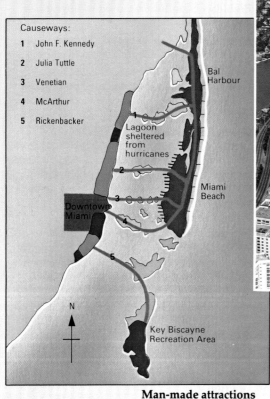

△ **Figure 14.15** Miami Beach, showing the sandy beaches backed by luxury hotels. Behind those is the lagoon with its marinas, and on the mainland, large private houses.

Figure 14.14 – Land use in Miami map legend:

Causeways:
1 John F. Kennedy
2 Julia Tuttle
3 Venetian
4 McArthur
5 Rickenbacker

Bal Harbour
Lagoon sheltered from hurricanes
Miami Beach
Downtown Miami
Key Biscayne Recreation Area

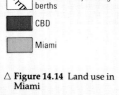

restored sandy beaches
luxury hotels with swimming pools
large private houses with swimming pools
open space
roads
marinas and yachting berths
CBD
Miami

△ **Figure 14.14** Land use in Miami

Man-made attractions

☐ Luxury hotels and private luxury flats which have been built on the sandbar (see Figures 14.14 and 14.15).

☐ Artificial islands formed by dredging the lagoon.

☐ Creation of large marinas in the lagoon.

☐ Improved roads and greater car ownership, which make travel easier from the industrial areas in the north.

☐ An international airport, one of the busiest in the world, making journeys from North America and North-West Europe less than half a day in duration.

☐ Wide range of entertainments, e.g. nightclubs, aquariums, marinas, saunas, zoos and golf courses.

Figure 14.12 map legend:

sandy beaches
state boundary
city
major tourist attraction
national or state forest
national seashore
national wildlife refuge
main road
National Park

0   200 km

Jacksonville
Marineland
Canaveral
Kennedy Space Cen
Disney World Orlando
Tampa
Circus World
St Petersburg
Lake Okeechobee
West Pa Beach
Tropical Aquariu
Fort Lauderda
Gulfstrea Park
Miami
Everglades National Park
Seaquariu
Coral Islands
Key West
Great White Heron

△ **Figure 14.12** Tourist attractions in Florida

	April	May	June	July	Aug.	Sept.
Average monthly temperature (°C)	25	28	30	31	31	30
Average hours of sunshine	9	9	8	8	8	7

△ **Figure 14.13** 'Sunny Florida' (Miami)

☐ Nearness to other attractions, e.g. Disney World, the Kennedy Space Centre, the Everglades and the coral islands of Key West (Figure 14.12).

Disney World – 'an international centre'

Near the town of Orlando (Figure 14.12) is 'Walt Disney World' – a totally human creation. Opened in 1971, it covers over 100 km² and consists of reclaimed swamps, lake and forest. The swamp was drained and replaced with clear water, while artificial hills made the relief more interesting. The complex includes air-conditioned buildings, a gas-fired power station and a water purification plant. The number of visitors from all over the world grew from 9 million in 1979 to 14 million in 1982. The 'Experimental Prototype Community of Tomorrow' ('EPCOT') centre (see Figure 14.16) opened in 1982 with 'a new concept of international understanding by presenting exhibitions on the differing cultures of mankind'. Virtually every package holiday from North America and Europe includes a stay at Orlando. Figure 14.16 shows the layout of this 'self-contained' resort.

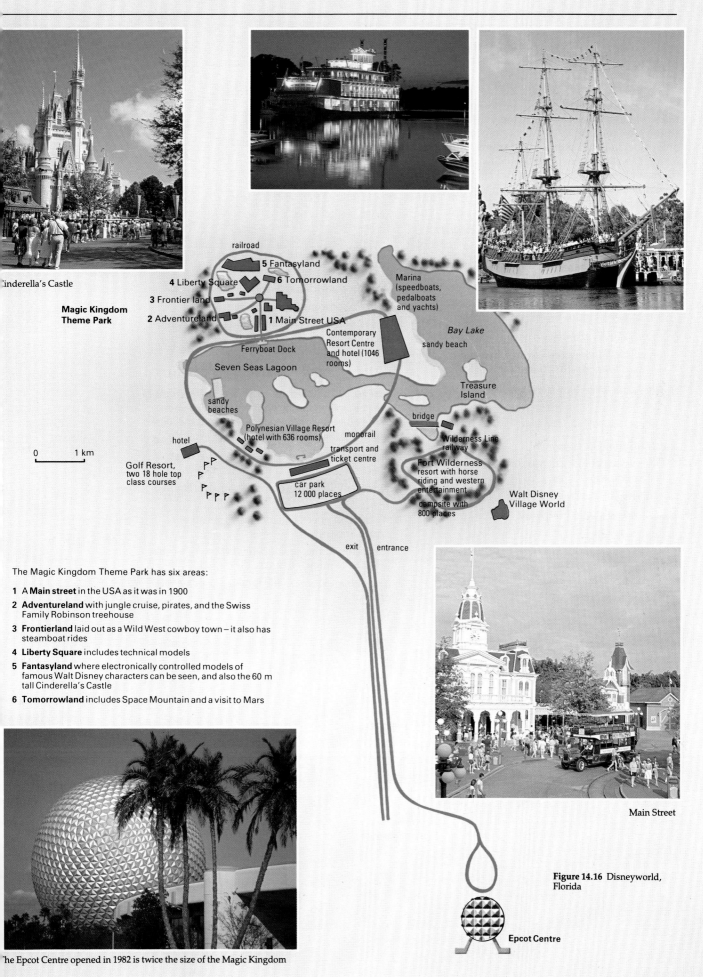

Cinderella's Castle

Magic Kingdom Theme Park

railroad

5 Fantasyland
4 Liberty Square   **6** Tomorrowland
3 Frontier land
2 Adventureland   **1** Main Street USA

Ferryboat Dock

Seven Seas Lagoon

Contemporary Resort Centre and hotel (1046 rooms)

Marina (speedboats, pedalboats and yachts)

Bay Lake
sandy beach

Treasure Island

sandy beaches

bridge

Polynesian Village Resort (hotel with 636 rooms)

Wilderness Line railway

hotel

monorail transport and ticket centre

Fort Wilderness resort with horse riding and western entertainment campsite with 800 places

Walt Disney Village World

Golf Resort, two 18 hole top class courses

0   1 km

car park 12 000 places

exit   entrance

The Magic Kingdom Theme Park has six areas:

1 A **Main street** in the USA as it was in 1900

2 **Adventureland** with jungle cruise, pirates, and the Swiss Family Robinson treehouse

3 **Frontierland** laid out as a Wild West cowboy town – it also has steamboat rides

4 **Liberty Square** includes technical models

5 **Fantasyland** where electronically controlled models of famous Walt Disney characters can be seen, and also the 60 m tall Cinderella's Castle

6 **Tomorrowland** includes Space Mountain and a visit to Mars

Main Street

Figure 14.16 Disneyworld, Florida

Epcot Centre

The Epcot Centre opened in 1982 is twice the size of the Magic Kingdom

Tourism in developing countries

Governments of developing countries have seen the world tourist industry growing, and several countries (especially in the Mediterranean region of Europe) improving their standards of living as a result. Developing countries would like to use tourism to try to break their 'vicious circle of poverty', and the profits would help to pay for new industries, housing and services.

Attractions of the West Indies as a tourist area

The natural environment

☐ The climate is sunny and much warmer (especially in winter) than in North America and Europe (Figure 14.18).

☐ The scenery is attractive – usually either –
  (a) volcanic mountains covered in forest, or
  (b) coral islands with sandy beaches.

☐ The warm, clear blue seas are ideal for water sports.

☐ There is varied wild life.

The traditional environment

☐ Different customs (calypsos, steel bands), food, festivals and carnivals.

☐ Cultural and historic resorts.

Amenities created for tourism

☐ Luxury hotels.

☐ Air transport and airports, so that all parts of North America and Western Europe are now within a few hours' flight (Figure 14.17).

☐ Facilities for cruise liners.

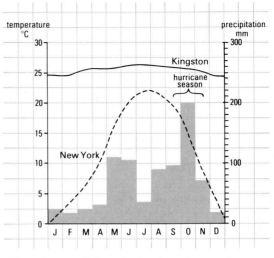

◁ **Figure 14.18** Kingston, Jamaica

Changing conditions in developed countries

☐ Increased income and more leisure time.

☐ A desire to travel further afield and to try new recreational activities.

Advantages and disadvantages of tourism

Figure 14.20 summarises some of the attractions of tourism to a developing country, but also shows that not all of the improvements benefit the local community (Figure 14.19).

Problems in developing tourism in the West Indies

☐ Hurricanes can cause severe damage (Figure 2.11).

☐ Rises in oil prices will increase both air and cruise liner prices.

☐ Recession in the developed world reduces the amount of money to spare for tourism.

☐ The demand for specific types of holiday may change.

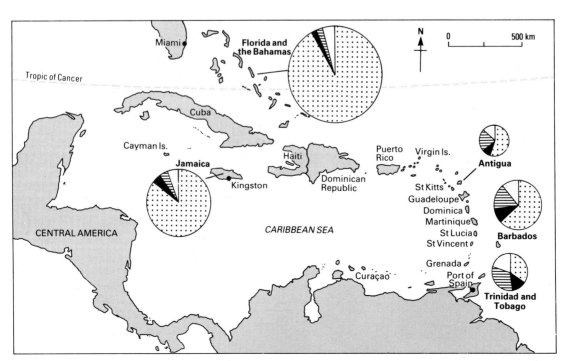

◁ **Figure 14.17** Origin of tourists in the West Indies

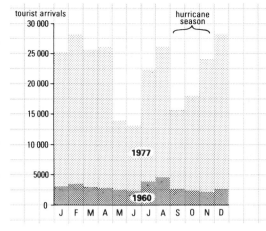

△ **Figure 14.21** Tourist arrivals in Barbados

Figure 14.19 Haiti – the poor local population live in squalor while the tourists benefit from development

Planning for the future

It is considered that tourism provides a weak base upon which to build the economy of a country. However, those countries which do have natural attractions should be encouraged to develop tourism, providing that the profits are used to try to raise the standard of living of all the islanders, and that the environment is not spoilt in the process.

Figure 14.20 Tourism in the developing world

Advantages

Uses physical environment to bring in capital (sun, sea, sand and scenery)

Increased income from tourism can be greater than that from the export of a few raw materials

Creates domestic employment, especially for the younger age groups, in entertainment, as hotel waiters, cleaners, and guides. One hotel of 300 beds can create 100 local jobs

Reduces the depopulation of islands

Encourages local craft industries e.g. fabrics, ceramics, leather-work, and woodwork

Creates a local market for farm produce

Overseas money builds airports, roads and hotels

Income gained can increase local amenities e.g. tarred roads, electricity, schools and hospitals

Increased links with other countries and an increased prestige in the world

Disadvantages

Pollution and destruction of natural environment; noise, litter, crime, vandalism and visual

Only thirteen developing countries earn over 10% of their foreign income from tourism; Barbados with 41% and Mexico with 26% are the two highest

The income per person from tourism is only about 10% of that in a developed country

Many hotels are foreign owned and profits go overseas to tour operators, travel agencies and airlines. Tourists spend most money in hotels and so do not benefit the local community

Possible seasonal unemployment (Figure 14.21)

Farming economy is damaged as land is sold to developers (locals cannot afford increased land prices), and farmers look for higher paid jobs in hotels

Much food used in hotels is imported

Building hotels forces some locals to move

Money borrowed from overseas increases the countries' debts, and that used to build hotels and airports could have been used for local houses and roads

Destruction or commercialisation of traditional cultures

Increased contact with outside world can lead to social problems e.g. crime, drugs

RECREATION AND TOURISM
Tourism in Barbados

Barbados is located 13° North of the Equator in the trade wind belt (Figure 14.17). It is the most easterly of the West Indian islands, and its year round sunshine and its temperature of between 24°C and 25°C day and night, summer and winter, make it ideal for tourists. Being an island also prevents the excessive heat and humidity of many other tropical areas. There is also a wide range of scenery including:

☐ The mountainous interior.

☐ The sheltered west coast with its sandy beaches overlooking the Caribbean Sea (Figure 14.22). Bridgetown, the capital, is located here.

☐ The more exposed east coast with its rolling Atlantic breakers.

Three types of tourist development

1 The large hotel with all amenities on the spot. Hotels such as the one shown in Figure 14.22 aim to provide maximum comfort and are situated as near as possible to the best beaches.

   1 Why is Tamarind Cove a good site for a hotel?

   2 What extra facilities have been laid on for tourists?

   3 Which is the most expensive season at the hotel and why is it?

2 The holiday village complex This is a new type of development taking place on several West Indian islands. The idea is to disperse the accommodation and amenities, and to try to integrate the whole with the natural environment. One such village-type development is described in Figure 14.23.

   1 How does it fit in with the local environment?

   2 Why might some tourists prefer to stay here rather than in the luxury hotels?

   3 Attempt to draw a plan to show the layout of Barbados Beach Village.

3 Facilities for cruise liner passengers

The rise in popularity of cruise liners has grown considerably since 1960.

   Often liners will anchor in Bridgetown harbour for a single day. In this time passengers will probably be hurried around the more exotic parts of the island and buy local souvenirs before sailing on to the next port. The amount of money spent is therefore limited.

   Occasionally, however, liners will make a break of several days in the middle of their voyage for passengers to 'relax and explore' Barbados (Figure 14.24). These passengers will spend more money but, as with those staying in luxury hotels, most of the income goes to the hoteliers rather than to the islanders (page 115). Using Figure 14.24,

   1 Why is Bridgetown a good stopping point?

   2 What are the advantages and disadvantages of a cruise liner visiting Barbados?

The hotel in the photograph is medium sized with a quiet, relaxed informal atmosphere.

Location	The hotel is situated on the beautiful west coast of the island, next to an excellent beach.
Accommodation	55 fully air-conditioned rooms with view of beach (superior rooms) or pool (standard rooms). All rooms have their own bath or shower. The hotel has a large dining room, several bars and is air-conditioned.
Facilities	Water-skiing, skin-diving, windsurfing and sailing are available on the beach next to the hotel. The hotel has its own swimming pool, and offers golf and tennis at nearby locations and also evening entertainments.

Departures on or between		Jan. 1 – Mar. 31	Apr. 1 – June 30	July 1 – Aug. 31	Sept. 1 – Nov. 30
Number of nights in hotel	7	£ 775	£ 545	£ 595	£ 575
	14	975	745	795	775
Supplements per person per night for superior room		8	4	8	4
Child reduction		25%	25%	25%	25%

Supplement information for additional nights (over 14) available on request.

△ **Figure 14.22** Tamarind Cove – a hotel in Barbados

The beach village complex is a less conventional form of hotel consisting of small villas and bungalows set amid palms and shrubs, and located very close to the beach. The village provides a mixture of self-catering accommodation and conventional hotel rooms which are situated away from the beach in the hotel gardens. There is a full restaurant and there are also self-service snack bars. The village is not luxurious or sophisticated but informal and relaxed and ideally suited to families.

Deep sea fishing, scuba-diving, snorkelling, sailing and water-skiing can all be arranged from the village, and golf and tennis are available nearby. There is a freshwater swimming pool situated away from the beach, and the village also has a night club.

THE ITINERARY

Day 1 Sat.

Depart Gatwick on morning flight, arrive San Juan in afternoon, transfer to cruise liner and sail at 20.30 hours.

Day 2 Sun. to Day 4 Tues. Cruising

Docking at La Guaira on Mon. and Grenada on Tues.

Day 5 Weds.

Arrival in Barbados in morning, transfer to exclusive hotel a few miles from Bridgetown where the next seven nights will be spent. The hotel is fully modernised and has a swimming pool, tennis courts and private beach with watersports facilities. All rooms have their own bathrooms and are fully air-conditioned.

Day 12 Weds.

Rejoin the cruise liner for evening sailing.

Day 13 Thurs. and 14 Fri. Cruising

Docking at St Lucia on Thurs. and St Thomas on Fri.

Day 15 Sat.

Arrival in San Juan in morning, transfer to hotel for one night.

Day 16 Sun.

Late morning flight to Gatwick.

△ **Figure 14.23** Barbados Beach Village (top)   △ **Figure 14.24** Cruising in the Caribbean

THE ENVIRONMENT
Problems within the Americas

The soil

Only 30 per cent of the earth's surface is land, and only 11 per cent of this is classed as prime agricultural land. It can take 100 to 400 years to produce 10 mm of soil, and between 3000 and 12 000 years to produce a sufficient depth for farming. Yet, as Figure 15.1 shows, human development is ruining this essential ingredient; indeed it is estimated that by A.D. 2000 one-third of the area now ploughed will have been reduced to dust.

Examples of soil losses in the Americas

□ Gulleys formed in areas such as the Tennessee Valley from the clearance of trees (page 81).

□ Exposed soil blown away (Figure 15.2), leaving the 'dust bowl', which stretches from Texas into Canada (page 24).

□ Irrigation leading, as in California, to increased salinity (page 69).

□ Overcultivation by one crop (e.g. cotton in the USA) or the intensification of farming in an area (California).

□ Overgrazing by animals in the American Mid-West and the grasslands of South America.

□ Shifting cultivation in the tropics, causing the heavy rainfall to leach out minerals in the areas of cleared forest (page 17).

□ Urbanisation, especially by the fast growing cities of Latin America.

Forests

Estimates (page 71) suggest that 14 hectares of forests are being cleared in the world every minute, the largest proportion being in the rain forests of Brazil and Central America. The consequences of these clearances are explained on page 120.

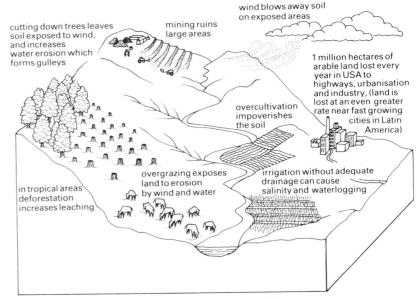

△ **Figure 15.1** Causes of soil loss

▽ **Figure 15.2** Large open fields means that exposed soil is easily blown away

Wildlife

In 1980 2000 vertebrate animals were listed as endangered species, along with many other plants and insects.

□ Bison were estimated to number 60 million when Europeans landed in North America. By 1890 only some 300 were left – the rest having been slaughtered for meat, hides and sport (Figures 15.3 and 15.4).

□ The vicuna, which is the national emblem of Peru, has just become a protected species.

□ The American alligator had its numbers reduced by 98 per cent between 1960 and 1972 and is near to extinction.

□ Mexican grizzly bears survive on only one isolated ranch.

□ Giant armadillos (Brazil), green turtles (West Indies), the Californian condor and Pampas deer are all also virtually extinct.

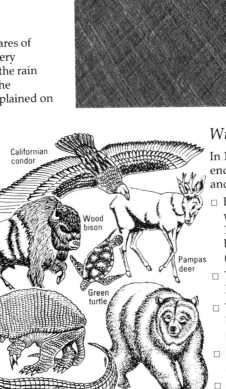

- distribution in 1980
- distribution in 1890
- distribution in 1800

△ **Figure 15.3** Distribution of the American Wood bison

▷ **Figure 15.4** Endangered species in the Americas

Californian condor
Wood bison
Pampas deer
Green turtle
Giant armadillo
American alligator
Mexican grizzly

The air

□ Smog is the polluted form of fog, and is caused by industrial smoke and automobile exhausts. Los Angeles is often covered by smog. Figure 15.5 describes conditions in Lima.

□ The 'greenhouse effect' is the scientific explanation of the consequences of carbon dioxide (CO^2) being released into the air by the burning of wood and such fossil fuels as coal and oil. This build-up allows the sun's heat to reach the earth, but prevents heat loss back into space. The amount of CO^2 in the air could double between 1980 and A.D. 2000, and this could increase the world's temperatures, reduce rainfall and cause polar ice to melt (Figure 15.6).

□ Acid rain is of recent worldwide concern. Rain turns acid when sulphur and nitrogen oxides are released from ore smelters, power stations and automobiles. Mixed with water vapour, these pollutants can increase the acidity of rain by 40 per cent (Figure 15.7).

△ **Figure 15.5** Smog in Lima (*Geographical Magazine*)

▷ **Figure 15.6** The greenhouse effect (right)

▽ **Figure 15.7** The Acid rain cycle in north east USA and Canada (below)

▽ **Figure 15.8** Water pollution – an example of how pollutants build up in a wildlife chain. Excessive levels of nitrates and phosphates can also pollute water, often causing 'algal blooms' which must then be cleared. Such high levels also reduce animal and plant species found in lakes and rivers (bottom)

▷ **Figure 15.9** The effects of pollution in Lake Erie (far right)

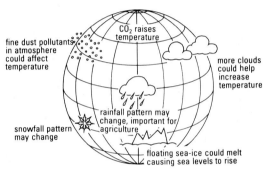

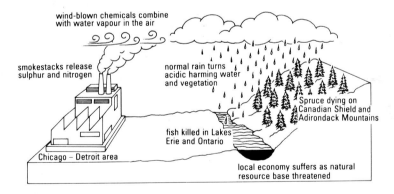

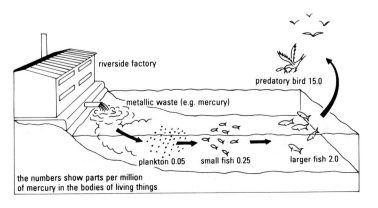

Water

Polluted water is responsible for many diseases, including typhoid, dysentery and cholera (page 62).

In the Great Lakes region of North America, various pollutants have made Lake Erie a 'dead lake'. *'One of the Nation's most polluted streams, Ohio's Cuyahoga became so covered with oil and debris that in July 1969 the river caught fire in Cleveland's factory area, damaging two railway bridges. Along this six-mile stretch, before emptying into Lake Erie, the river receives the wastes of steel mills, chemical and meat-rendering plants, and other industries. Just upstream, Cleveland and Akron discharge inadequately treated sewage. And from hinterland farms drain phosphate- and nitrate-rich fertilizers and poisonous pesticides (Figure 15.8).*

'The Cuyahoga flows into Lake Erie, mixing with effluent from the Detroit and Maumee Rivers. The flow, rich in nutrients, stimulates growth of Cladophora algae. As the overfertilized algae die and decompose, oxygen essential to fish life is depleted (Figure 15.9). Lake Erie is said to be ''too thick to drink, too thin to plough''.'

Minerals

Three overriding concerns are:

(a) The exhaustion of resources, of both energy and minerals.

(b) The dumping of industrial wastes, which may vary from radio-active nuclear waste from power stations to slag heaps and dangerous chemicals.

(c) Oil spillage.

Conclusions

It is the developed countries which tend to prevent conservation because they have most to lose, while in the developing world a hungry person eats first and thinks of the environment second. There is a need for a world conservation plan, but environmental organisations lack political power. Do you agree with the statement, 'Pollution is the result of both the progress of the rich and the poverty of the poor'?

Economic gain – environmental loss

The Amazon Forest

The current annual rate of deforestation in the Amazon Forest covers an area larger than Wales. Deforestation ignores the fact that life can only exist on earth through the oxygen given out by trees. The forest is being cleared for short-term economic gains with no thought for the future – once destroyed it can never be replaced (Figure 15.10 and page 71).

Deforestation can lead to:

☐ An upset in the oxygen balance by which we would produce too much CO^2 (Figure 15.11).

☐ Too much CO^2 affecting the world's climate – less evapotranspiration from trees can mean drought, too much CO^2 might absorb heat from the sun possibly causing a mini-iceage, or might raise the temperature of the atmosphere, melting the polar icecaps.

☐ Loss of wildlife and trees.

☐ Impoverishment and loss of soil.

☐ Effects upon Indian tribes whereby the cultural shock (page 33) has decimated their numbers.

▽ **Figure 15.10** The Amazon forest, economic gain – environmental loss

CO_2 given off

O_2 absorbed

CO_2 absorbed by trees

photosynthesis

O_2 given off

climatic change due to more CO_2 – higher temperatures ? – drought ? – mini iceage ?

more CO_2 given off

increase in industry

burning trees give off CO_2

less O_2 available yet increasing world population needs more

forest being cut down, and burnt fewer trees to absorb CO_2

fewer trees give off less O_2

△ **Figure 15.11** The oxygen balance

a) One oak tree provides enough O_2 for two humans per day

b) One football pitch takes one week to produce enough O_2 for 75 spectators for one match

c) 150 oak trees replaces the CO_2 produced by one small car with O_2

1 What is the value of the Amazon rainforest as it stands today?

2 What short-term economic gains are being made by deforestation?

3 What long-term environmental losses are being made by destroying the Amazon rainforest?

Forested area

cumulo nimbus clouds

evapotranspiration from trees adds moisture to the air

Heavy convectional storms most afternoons

forested slopes, nature in balance

habitat for wildlife (birds, animals and insects)

shifting cultivators live in harmony with nature, only limited deforestation in Amazonia for fuel

fragile soils shielded from heavy rain by trees

movement of rain-water through soil regulates river flow, prevents flooding and stores water for drier periods

clean river useable for drinking

tree roots control flow of water and stabilise the soil preventing landslides

little economic gain
considerable environmental gain

Deforested area

fewer trees mean less evapotranspiration

ranching
mainly for poor quality meat for hamburgers and frankfurters

plantation crops

heavy rainfall (both in amount and intensity) washes away the unprotected surface soil

timber
loss of wildlife and many species of trees

highways

mining

lack of trees creates a fuel shortage

rapid surface runoff causes gulley erosion and flooding

muddy water undrinkable

no roots to hold soil together results in landslides

heavy rainfall causes leaching ruining the soil

silt blocks rivers and fills reservoirs

reasonable short term economic gain
considerable environmental loss

The Alaskan pipeline

The Alaskan oilfield, discovered in 1968, is the largest in North America. The oil was essential to the energy-consuming USA, but before it could be used a way had to be found of transporting it south. There were two possible routes:

(a) By tanker from Prudhoe Bay (Figure 15.13); but the Beaufort Sea is frozen for most of the year, the route is dangerous and would have needed too many tankers, and the risk of spillage was too great.

(b) A pipeline 1300 km southwards to the ice-free port of Valdez. This had to be built against great difficulties (Figure 15.12) and to the satisfaction of a highly organised lobby of conservationists.

◁ **Figure 15.12** The Alaskan pipeline

▽ **Figure 15.13** Physical problems which faced the builders of the Alaskan pipeline

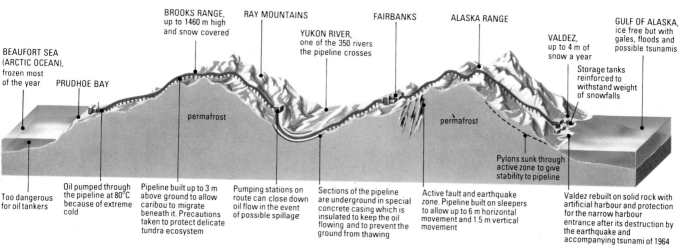

BEAUFORT SEA (ARCTIC OCEAN), frozen most of the year

PRUDHOE BAY

BROOKS RANGE, up to 1460 m high and snow covered

RAY MOUNTAINS

YUKON RIVER, one of the 350 rivers the pipeline crosses

FAIRBANKS

ALASKA RANGE

VALDEZ, up to 4 m of snow a year

GULF OF ALASKA, ice free but with gales, floods and possible tsunamis

Storage tanks reinforced to withstand weight of snowfalls

permafrost

permafrost

Pylons sunk through active zone to give stability to pipeline

Too dangerous for oil tankers

Oil pumped through the pipeline at 80°C because of extreme cold

Pipeline built up to 3 m above ground to allow caribou to migrate beneath it. Precautions taken to protect delicate tundra ecosystem

Pumping stations on route can close down oil flow in the event of possible spillage

Sections of the pipeline are underground in special concrete casing which is insulated to keep the oil flowing and to prevent the ground from thawing

Active fault and earthquake zone. Pipeline built on sleepers to allow up to 6 m horizontal movement and 1.5 m vertical movement

Valdez rebuilt on solid rock with artificial harbour and protection for the narrow harbour entrance after its destruction by the earthquake and accompanying tsunami of 1964

Problems facing the pipeline and its builders

Climate and latitude

□ Air temperatures fall to −50°C, which causes frostbite and makes working less efficient.

□ Machines have to be run all the time to prevent them freezing.

□ In winter there are up to 22 hours of darkness per day.

□ Permafrost makes it difficult to dig into the soil, and in summer the surface melting (active zone – see Figure 2.27) can cause the pipeline to sag and threaten breaking.

Physical

□ The oil has to be pumped at 80°C to prevent it freezing and to enable it to flow.

□ The pipeline has to be insulated to prevent the contents freezing when it is overground, and to prevent the ground thawing when it is underground, which could lead to sagging and fracture.

□ It has to rise to 1460 m to cross the Brooks Range (Figure 15.13).

□ It has to cross over 350 rivers and streams.

□ It has to cross the earthquake zone of the Alaskan Range.

□ The site of Valdez had to be moved after the 1964 earthquake (page 12), and the oil terminal now stands on bedrock hopefully above the level of tsunamis (tidal waves).

□ The Valdez narrows are only 1000 m wide and, together with fogs and high winds, the route is dangerous for large tankers.

Conservation problems

□ There was concern because once the tundra vegetation is removed regeneration is exceptionally slow.

□ The pipeline crossed the caribou migration routes, a problem overcome by raising it on stilts.

□ Other animals whose habitats were affected included foxes, wolves, bears, moose and dall sheep.

□ There was concern over oil spillage which would affect both vegetation and wildlife in an area of adverse physical conditions. Figure 15.13 shows some of the ways in which these problems have been, hopefully, overcome.

Methods and problems

The developing countries, often relying upon one or two primary products for their income, are falling further and further behind the developed countries (Figure 16.1). As the trade gap (pages 94–5) widens, it means that the developing countries have less money to –

(a) buy goods from the developed world or indeed from other developing countries, and

(b) develop their own industries and improve their own communications, farming, health, schools, housing, water supplies, soil management and energy supplies.

If a developing country wishes to develop it has to borrow money. Figure 16.2 shows the scale of borrowing made by countries in Latin America. Aid can come from three sources.

Bilateral aid This is government-to-government aid which goes direct from one developed country to a developing country. In 1960 60 per cent of aid came from this source, but only 30 per cent in 1980. The recipient country puts forward a development plan, which, if accepted, will be finalised, equipped and operated by the donor country. Although this method is quick to implement and credit rates may be low, it has disadvantages in that the technology given is often unsuitable and linked to a particular project, and the recipient country has to buy goods from its donor country. One example of this 'economic colonialism' was when the USA gave Peru large loans to help explore for oil. In return Peru had to buy jet aircraft from the USA, allow the USA to fish in Peruvian waters and export to the USA a high percentage of any oil discovered.

Multinational aid This type of aid comes from such international agencies as the World Bank, the International Monetary Fund, the Food and Agriculture Organisation (FAO) and UNESCO. By 1980 over 66 per cent of aid came from this source, with the advantage of having no political ties and not being linked to specific projects. However, the amount of aid available is too limited, much time is lost in organising projects, and the interest rates put the recipient deeper into debt (Figure 16.3), though the poorest borrowers do get interest-free loans which can be repaid over a 50-year period.

Charities Such voluntary organisations as Oxfam and Christian Aid raise money in the developed world to support projects in the poorer countries. Again no political ties are made, and projects are on a smaller and more realistic scale.

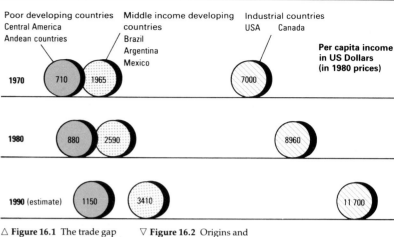

△ **Figure 16.1** The trade gap between the developed and developing countries

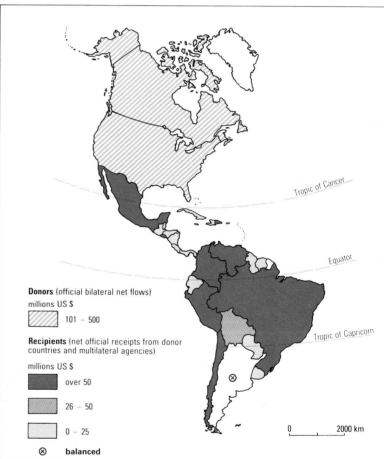

▽ **Figure 16.2** Origins and directions of aid, annual averages

▷ **Figure 16.3** Debts owed by Latin American countries, billions US $

rank order in World 1982	country	debt owed	
		1980	1982
1	Brazil	60	87
2	Mexico	55	81
3	Argentina	27	37
4	Venezuela	18	36
9	Chile	11	18
10	Peru	7	12
12	Colombia	4	7

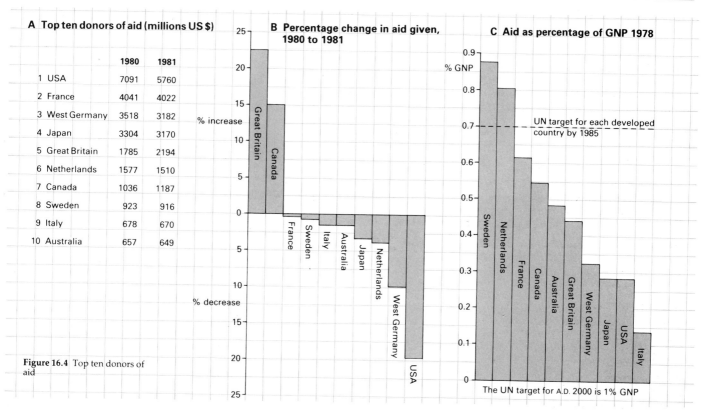

A Top ten donors of aid (millions US $)

		1980	1981
1	USA	7091	5760
2	France	4041	4022
3	West Germany	3518	3182
4	Japan	3304	3170
5	Great Britain	1785	2194
6	Netherlands	1577	1510
7	Canada	1036	1187
8	Sweden	923	916
9	Italy	678	670
10	Australia	657	649

Figure 16.4 Top ten donors of aid

B Percentage change in aid given, 1980 to 1981

C Aid as percentage of GNP 1978

UN target for each developed country by 1985

The UN target for A.D. 2000 is 1% GNP

In 1980 the Brandt Report (see page 126) said:
'Economic growth of one country depends increasingly upon the performance of others. The South cannot grow adequately without the North – the North cannot prosper unless there is greater progress in the South.'

What are the basic problems?

☐ The countries that borrow money fall deeper into debt, especially those which have borrowed most, such as Brazil and Mexico (Figure 16.3).

☐ World interest rates are tending to increase.

☐ In times of recession in the developed world, the amount of aid given is reduced (Figures 16.4A and 16.4B). The United Nations have set a target for developed countries to give 0.7 per cent of their GNP to developing countries by 1985, and 1 per cent by A.D. 2000. Figure 16.4C shows how far most countries are from fulfilling this aim.

☐ Also in times of recession, the developed countries try to protect their own industries from cheap imports from the developing countries (Figure 16.5A). Development agencies recommend free trade between the North and the South as a way to overcome recession and unemployment (Figure 16.5B).

☐ A new, single currency is needed for the whole world.

Conclusion

Should the North help the South by giving aid and encouraging industries even if it means higher unemployment and a lower standard of living in the North, or is it just the South's hard luck?

Figure 16.5 Aid, or protectionism?

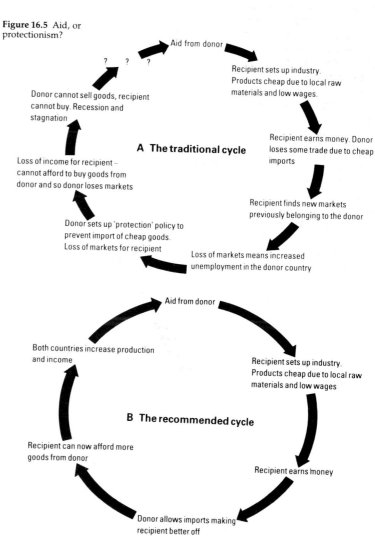

NORTH — SOUTH
GNP and Population

The GNP only indicates the average income per person, and it disguises just how poor the poorest are in terms of their standard of living.

▽ **Figure 17.1** Population data for the Americas, 1980

number on map	country	population estimate (millions)	crude birth rate	crude death rate	number of years to double population	estimated populaton in A.D. 2000 (millions)	infant mortality rate (per 1000 births up to 1 year old)	% population under 15 years old	life expectancy at birth (years)	GNP US $
1	Canada	24.1	15	7	89	26.9	12	25	74	9650
2	United States	229.8	16	9	95	258.9	13	22	74	10 820
3	Belize	0.2	40	12	25	0.2	–	49	–	1030
4	Costa Rica	2.3	32	4	25	3.5	22	39	70	1810
5	El Salvador	4.9	39	7	22	8.7	53	45	63	570
6	Guatemala	7.5	43	12	22	12.8	69	45	58	1020
7	Honduras	3.9	47	12	20	7.1	103	48	57	530
8	Mexico	69.3	33	8	28	101.8	70	42	65	1590
9	Nicaragua	2.5	47	12	20	4.6	122	48	55	660
10	Panama	1.9	28	6	31	2.7	47	43	70	1350
11	Bahamas	0.3	22	5	41	0.4	28	44	69	2780
12	Barbados	0.3	16	8	80	0.3	27	32	70	2400
13	Cuba	9.8	15	6	77	12.3	19	32	72	1410
14	Dominica	0.1	21	5	43	0.1	20	–	58	410
15	Dominican Republic	5.6	37	9	25	8.5	96	45	60	990
16	Grenada	0.1	24	7	39	0.1	15	–	63	630
17	Guadeloupe	0.3	17	6	65	0.4	35	32	69	3260
18	Haiti	6.0	42	16	26	9.9	130	41	51	260
19	Jamaica	2.2	27	6	33	2.8	16	43	70	1246
20	Martinique	0.3	16	7	80	0.3	15	33	69	4680
21	Netherlands Antilles	0.3	28	7	32	0.4	25	38	62	3540
22	Puerto Rico	3.2	22	6	44	4.1	18	34	74	2970
23	St Lucia	0.1	32	7	29	0.1	33	50	67	780
24	St Vincent and the Grenadines	0.1	35	7	25	0.1	38	–	67	490
25	Trinidad and Tobago	1.2	26	6	36	1.4	24	33	69	3390
26	Bolivia	5.5	44	19	28	8.9	168	42	51	550
27	Brazil	121.4	32	8	29	198.5	84	41	64	1690
28	Colombia	27.8	29	8	33	42.8	77	41	62	1010
29	Ecuador	8.2	42	10	22	14.5	70	45	60	1050
30	Guyana	0.8	28	7	33	1.2	46	44	69	570
31	Paraguay	3.3	34	7	26	5.5	58	44	64	1060
32	Peru	18.1	39	12	26	29.3	92	42	56	730
33	Surinam	0.4	30	7	30	0.8	30	51	67	2360
34	Venezuela	15.5	36	6	23	25.9	45	42	66	3130
35	Argentina	28.2	25	9	43	33.8	41	28	69	2280
36	Chile	11.2	22	7	47	14.7	38	34	67	1690
37	Uruguay	2.9	20	10	67	3.5	48	27	71	2090
–	(United Kingdom)	55.9	13	12	693	57.1	13	22	73	6340

The number for each country (column 1) is the same as on the map in Figure 17.2

1–2 North America,
3–10 Central America,

11–25 Caribbean,
26–37 South America

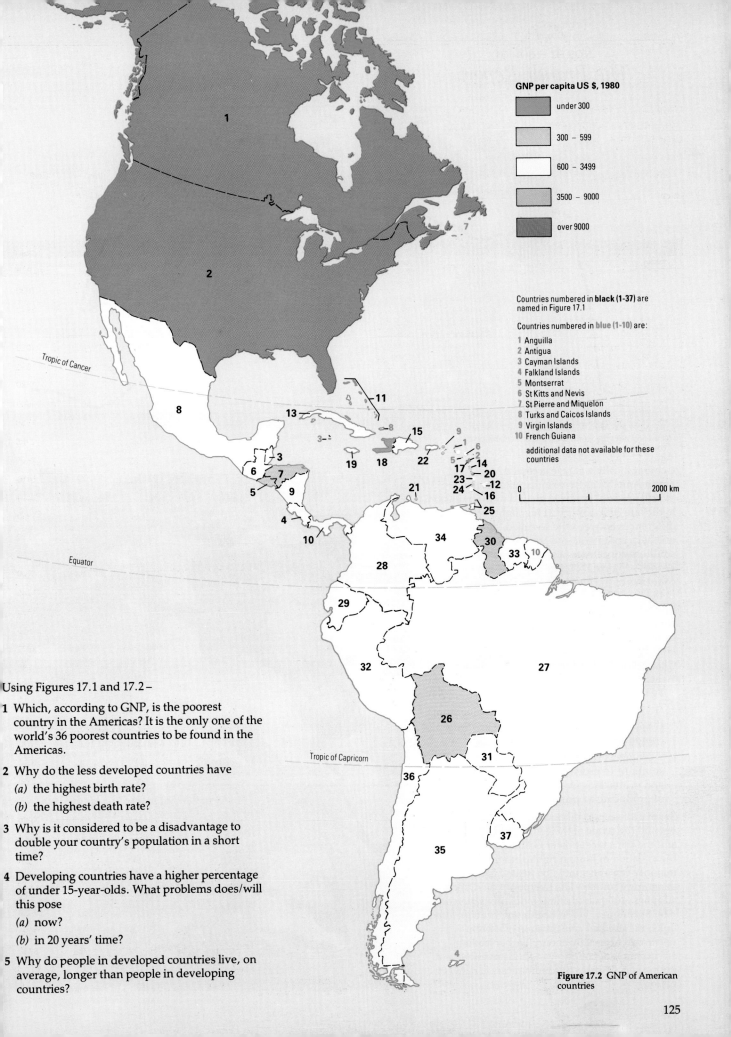

GNP per capita US $, 1980

- under 300
- 300 – 599
- 600 – 3499
- 3500 – 9000
- over 9000

Countries numbered in **black (1-37)** are named in Figure 17.1

Countries numbered in blue (1-10) are:

1 Anguilla
2 Antigua
3 Cayman Islands
4 Falkland Islands
5 Montserrat
6 St Kitts and Nevis
7 St Pierre and Miquelon
8 Turks and Caicos Islands
9 Virgin Islands
10 French Guiana

additional data not available for these countries

0 ————————— 2000 km

Tropic of Cancer

Equator

Tropic of Capricorn

Using Figures 17.1 and 17.2 –

1 Which, according to GNP, is the poorest country in the Americas? It is the only one of the world's 36 poorest countries to be found in the Americas.

2 Why do the less developed countries have

   (a) the highest birth rate?

   (b) the highest death rate?

3 Why is it considered to be a disadvantage to double your country's population in a short time?

4 Developing countries have a higher percentage of under 15-year-olds. What problems does/will this pose

   (a) now?

   (b) in 20 years' time?

5 Why do people in developed countries live, on average, longer than people in developing countries?

Figure 17.2 GNP of American countries

The Brandt Report

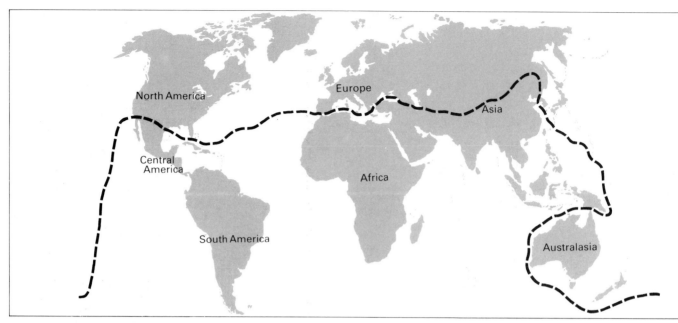

△ **Figure 17.3** North–South is a very simple way of showing how the world divides into rich and poor countries

Geographically we have accepted North and South America as two continents, but the term 'North – South' has been given a new dimension in the late 20th century. It highlights the differences between the so-called 'developed' northern continents and the less developed southern continents (also known as the Third World) – Figure 17.3. The gap between the countries of the North and the South was brought to the fore when the Brandt Report was published in 1980. The Report, entitled *North – South*, was compiled by an independent group of statesmen from most of the nations of the world, headed by Herr Willy Brandt (a former West German Chancellor) and including Britain's Edward Heath.

Two of the aims of the group were:

☐ 'To study the grave global issues arising from the social and economic disparities of the world community.'

☐ 'To suggest ways of promoting adequate solutions to problems involved in development and in attacking absolute poverty with the hope of producing a "programme for survival".'

Several key issues discussed in the Report lie beyond the scope of the geographer (disarmament and the arms race, power politics, corruption, and the violation of human rights) but the vast majority can and should be treated in a school geography course – like overpopulation, food supplies and malnutrition, industrialisation and new techniques, world health, international trade links, the use and conservation of natural resources (especially energy), urbanisation, environmental pollution and conservation, and improving all forms of communication between nations.

One aim of this book has been to provide background knowledge so that you can become aware of these international problems facing our present world and its future generations, and so that you may be better informed to help, even in a small way, to improve your world. In attempting to look at problem areas, examples have been taken from one so-called 'developed' continent – America *North* – and one so-called 'developing'

continent – America *South*. Yet hopefully it has shown that within North America there are deprived people and regions just as in parts of South America there is wealth and development uncharacteristic of the 'Third World'.

Figures 17.4, 17.5 and 17.6 illustrate some of the problems facing Latin America, whilst Figure 17.7 compares some of the differences between 'The North' and 'The South'.

▽ **Figure 17.7** Comparisons between the developed and developing worlds

	developed countries	developing countries
Gross National Product	majority over 5000 US $ per year; 80% of world's total income	majority under 2000 US $ per year; 20% of world's total income
population growth	relatively slow partly due to family planning; 25% of world's population; population doubles in 80 years	extremely fast, little or no family planning; 75% of world's population; population doubles in 30 years
housing	high standard of permanent housing; indoor amenities e.g. electricity, water supply and sewerage	low standard, mainly temporary housing; very rarely any amenities
types of jobs	manufacturing and service industries, (90% of world's manufacturing industry)	mainly in primary industries
levels of mechanisation	highly mechanised with new techniques, 96% of world spending on development projects and research	mainly hand labour or the use of animals
exports	manufactured goods	unprocessed raw materials
energy	high level of consumption; main sources are coal, oil, HEP and nuclear power	low level of consumption; wood still a major source
communications	motorways, railways and airports	road, rail and airports only near main cities, rural areas have little development
diet	balanced diet; several meals per day; high protein intake	unbalanced diet; 20% of population suffers from malnutrition; low protein intake
life expectancy	over 70 years	under 50 years
health service	very good, large numbers of doctors and good hospital facilities	very poor, few doctors and inadequate hospital facilities
education	majority have full time secondary education (16+)	very few have any formal education

◁ **Figure 17.4** Homelessness – people sleeping on warm air vents in Mexico City (opposite)

◁ **Figure 17.5** Over employment and lack of mechanisation in agriculture – Bolivia (lower left)

◁ **Figure 17.6** Lack of adequate modern public transport (upper left)

Index